A HANDBOOK OF MMPI GROUP PROFILES

A Handbook of
MMPI
Group Profiles

RICHARD I. LANYON

University of Minnesota Press, Minneapolis

Library of Congress Catalog Card Number: 68-55387

PUBLISHED IN GREAT BRITAIN, INDIA, AND PAKISTAN BY THE OXFORD UNIVERSITY PRESS, LONDON, BOMBAY, AND KARACHI, AND IN CANADA BY THE COPP CLARK PUBLISHING CO. LIMITED, TORONTO

Preface

DURING my internship in clinical psychology I spent considerable time abstracting clinical research data on commonly used psychological tests to serve as an aid to diagnostic practice. Several years later, when I was using some of these materials on the MMPI as a teaching aid in graduate classes in personality assessment, it was suggested that the general need for such research summaries would warrant the preparation of a book. The present volume is the outcome of that suggestion.

Grateful acknowledgment is made to the many authors whose research is abstracted to provide the body of the book. Responsibility for the accuracy of the abstracts is, of course, my own. Special thanks are due to those authors who supplied supplementary data.

I wish to express my appreciation to a number of other people who assisted in various ways. Alice Merrill Plutchok and Carol Vogel Hamilton performed some of the initial literature search. Mrs. Irene Pillar typed a preliminary draft of the book, which was circulated in dittoed form. A number of my professional colleagues gave valuable feedback on their reactions to this preliminary draft. Genevieve Lanyon typed most of the final manuscript, and Marjorie Schiffman drew the profile charts. I am especially indebted to Jeanne Sinnen of the University of Minnesota Press for her expert editorial work in handling the manuscript and in taking care of many problems of which I was not even aware.

Acknowledgment is made to the following publishers and authors for permission to use copyrighted material:

AMERICAN PSYCHOLOGICAL ASSOCIATION. *Journal of Abnormal and Social Psychology*: D. R. Peterson, Predicting hospitalization of psychiatric outpatients (1954, 49, 260–265); N. D. Sundberg, The use of the MMPI for cross-cultural personality study: a preliminary report on the German translation (1956, 52, 281–283). *Journal of Applied Psychology*: P. L. Brown and R. F. Berdie, Driver behavior and scores on the MMPI (1960, 44, 18–21); R. D. Norman and M. Redlo, MMPI personality patterns for various college major groups (1952, 36, 404–409). *Journal of Consulting Psychology*: M. Apfeldorf, J. L. Scheinker, and G. L. Whitman, MMPI responses of aged domiciled veterans with disciplinary records (1966, 30, 362); F. Barron, Some test correlates of response to psychotherapy (1953, 17, 235–241); A. H. Canter, MMPI profiles in multiple sclerosis (1951, 15, 253–256); R. B. Dean and H. Richardson, Analysis of MMPI profiles of 40 college-educated overt male homosexuals (1964, 28, 483–486); W. J. Eichman, Discrimination of female schizophrenics with configural analysis of the MMPI profile (1959, 23, 442–447); J. E. Exner, E. McDowell, J. Pabst, W. Stackman, and L. Kirk, On the detection of willful falsifications in the MMPI (1963, 27, 91–94); M. J. Feldman, The use of the MMPI profile for prognosis and evaluation of shock therapy (1952, 16, 376–382); H. Gilberstadt and E. Farkas, Another look at MMPI profile types in multiple sclerosis (1961, 25, 440–444); L. D. Goodstein and V. N. Rowley, A further study of MMPI differences between parents of disturbed and nondisturbed children (1961, 25, 460); H. M. Grayson and L. B. Olinger, Simulation of "normalcy" by psychiatric patients on the MMPI (1957, 21, 73–77); L. J. Hanvik, MMPI profiles in patients with low back pain (1951, 15, 350–353); H. Levitt and C. Fellner, MMPI profiles of three obesity subgroups (1965, 29, 91); T. Linde and C. H. Patterson, The MMPI in cerebral palsy (1958, 22, 210–212); S. Liverant, MMPI differences between parents of disturbed and nondisturbed children (1959, 23, 256–260); R. L. McDonald and M. D. Gynther, MMPI differences associated with sex, race, and class in two adolescent samples (1963, 27, 112–116); W. G. Miller and T. E. Hannum, Characteristics of homosexually involved incarcerated females (1963, 27, 277); J. J. Motto, The MMPI performance of veterans with organic and psychiatric disabilities (1958, 22, 304); J. E. Muthard, MMPI findings for cerebral palsied college students (1965, 29, 599); L. H. Muzekari, The MMPI in predicting treatment outcome in alcoholism (1965, 29, 281); D. R. Peterson, The diagnosis of subclinical schizophrenia (1954, 18, 198–200); M. H. Randolph, H. Richardson, and R. C. Johnson, A comparison of social and solitary male delinquents (1961, 25, 293–295); G. M. Rapaport, "Ideal Self" instructions, MMPI profile changes, and the prediction of clinical improvement (1958, 22, 459–463); P. P. Rempel, The use of multivariate statistical analysis of MMPI scores in the classification of delinquent and non-delinquent high school boys (1958, 22, 17–23); A. Rosen, Test-retest stability of MMPI scales for a psychiatric population (1953, 17, 217–221); A. Rosen, Differentiation of diagnostic groups by individual MMPI scales (1958, 22, 453–457); R. E. Schulman and P. London, Hypnotic susceptibility and MMPI profiles (1963, 27, 157–160); F. C. Shontz, MMPI responses of patients with multiple sclerosis (1955, 19, 74); P. L. Sullivan, C. Miller, and W. Smelser, Factors of length of stay and progress in psychotherapy (1958, 22, 1–9); P. L. Sullivan and G. S. Welsh, A technique for objective configurational analysis of MMPI profiles (1952, 16, 383–388); R. Taft, A cross-cultural comparison of the MMPI (1957, 21, 161–164); E. S. Taulbee and B. D. Sisson, Configurational analysis of MMPI profiles of psychiatric groups (1957, 21, 413–417); E. E. Wagner and R. D. Dobbins, MMPI profiles of parishioners seeking pastoral counseling (1967, 31, 83–84); J. B. Wattron, Validity of the Marsh-Hilliard-Liechti MMPI sexual deviation scale in a state prison population (1958, 22, 16). *Psychological Monographs*: P. A. Marks, An assessment of the diagnostic process in a child guidance setting (1961, 75, No. 3); W. Schofield, Changes in responses to the Minnesota Multiphasic Personality Inventory following certain therapies (1950, 64, No. 5).

CATHOLIC UNIVERSITY OF AMERICA PRESS. *Studies in Psychology and Psychiatry from the Catholic University of America*: W. C. Bier, A comparative study of a seminary group and four other groups on the Minnesota Multiphasic Personality Inventory (1948, 7, 1–107).

DUKE UNIVERSITY PRESS. *Journal of Personality*: A. B. Hood, A study of the relationship between physique and personality variables as measured by the MMPI (1963, 31, 97–107).

Educational and Psychological Measurement: E. Rosen and G. B. Rizzo, Preliminary standardization of the MMPI for use in Italy: a case study in intercultural and intracultural differences (1961, 21, 629–636); M.

Spiaggia, An investigation of the personality traits of art students (1950, 10, 285–293).

HARPER AND ROW (HOEBER MEDICAL DIVISION). *Psychosomatic Medicine*: B. C. Schiele and J. Brozek, "Experimental neurosis" resulting from semistarvation in man (1948, 10, 31–50).

Journal of Clinical Psychology: A. L. Andersen and L. J. Hanvik, The psychometric localization of brain lesions: the differential effect of frontal and parietal lesions on MMPI profiles (1950, 6, 177–180); J. C. Ball, Comparison of MMPI profile differences among Negro-white adolescents (1960, 16, 304–307); C. W. Cabeen and J. C. Coleman, Group therapy with sex offenders: description and evaluation of a group therapy program in an institutional setting (1961, 17, 122–129); G. Calden and J. E. Hokanson, The influence of age on MMPI responses (1959, 15, 194–195); A. Canter, C. W. Day, J. B. Imboden, and L. E. Cluff, The influence of age and health status on the MMPI scores of a normal population (1962, 28, 71–73); J. H. Clark, The relationship between MMPI scores and psychiatric classification of army general prisoners (1952, 8, 86–89); D. G. Doehring and R. M. Reitan, MMPI performance of aphasic and nonaphasic brain-damaged patients (1960, 16, 307–309); A. E. Eschenbach and L. Dupree, The influence of stress on MMPI scale scores (1959, 15, 42–45); B. G. Fricke, Conversion hysterics and the MMPI (1956, 12, 322–326); L. J. Hanvik and M. Byrum, MMPI profiles of parents of child psychiatric patients (1959, 15, 427–431); J. E. Hokanson and G. Calden, Negro-white differences on the MMPI (1960, 16, 32–33); J. F. Hooke and P. A. Marks, MMPI characteristics of pregnancy (1962, 18, 316–317); H. B. Hovey, Somatization and other neurotic reactions and MMPI profiles (1949, 5, 153–156); D. P. Hoyt and G. M. Sedlacek, Differentiating alcoholics from normals and abnormals with the MMPI (1958, 14, 69–73); W. A. Kennedy, MMPI profiles of gifted adolescents (1962, 18, 148–149); L. Kingsley, MMPI profiles of psychopaths and prisoners (1960, 16, 302–304); H. Klove and D. G. Doehring, MMPI in epileptic groups with differential etiology (1962, 18, 149–153); C. G. Lauterbach, W. Vogel, and J. Hart, Comparison of the MMPI's of male problem adolescents and their parents (1962, 18, 485–487); R. J. Lucero and W. C. Currens, Effects of clinical training on personality functioning of the minister (1964, 20, 147); C. Miller, C. Wertz, and S. Counts,

Racial differences on the MMPI (1961, 17, 159–161); J. H. Panton, MMPI profile configurations among crime classification groups (1959, 15, 305–308); J. H. Panton, The identification of habitual criminalism with the MMPI (1962, 18, 133–136); J. H. Panton, The identification of predispositional factors in self-mutilation within a state prison population (1962, 18, 63–67); A. Rosen, W. M. Hales, and R. M. Peek, Comparability of MMPI card and booklet forms for psychiatric patients (1958, 14, 387–388); V. N. Rowley and F. B. Stone, MMPI differences between emotionally disturbed and delinquent adolescents (1962, 18, 481–484); J. W. Shaffer, K. Y. Ota, and T. E. Hanlon, The comparative validity of several MMPI indices of severity of psychopathology (1964, 20, 467–473); R. J. Silver and L. K. Sines, MMPI characteristics of a state hospital population (1961, 17, 142–146); F. B. Stone and V. N. Rowley, MMPI differences between emotionally disturbed and delinquent adolescent girls (1963, 19, 227–230); W. M. Swenson, Structured personality testing in the aged: an MMPI study of the gerontic population (1961, 17, 302–304); A. H. Urmer, H. O. Black, and L. V. Wendland, A comparison of taped and booklet forms of the MMPI (1960, 16, 33–34); L. A. Wauck, Schizophrenia and the MMPI (1950, 6, 279–282); S. Wolf, W. R. Freinek, and J. W. Shaffer, Comparability of complete oral and booklet forms of the MMPI (1964, 20, 375–378); W. D. Wolking, W. Quast, and J. J. Lawton, MMPI profiles of the parents of behaviorally disturbed children and parents from the general population (1966, 22, 39–48).

Journal of Counseling Psychology: J. Butcher, B. Ball and E. Ray, Effects of socio-economic level on MMPI differences in Negro-white college students (1964, 11, 83–87); J. Drasgow and J. McKenzie, College transcripts, graduation, and the MMPI (1958, 5, 196–199).

THE JOURNAL PRESS. *Genetic Psychology Monographs*: N. L. Farberow, Personality patterns of suicidal mental patients (1950, 42, 3–80); R. Taft, A psychological assessment of professional actors and related professions (1961, 64, 309–383); D. N. Wiener, Personality characteristics of selected disability groups (1952, 45, 175–255). *Journal of General Psychology*: H. E. Hill,

C. A. Haertzen, and R. Glaser, Personality characteristics of narcotic addicts as indicated by the MMPI (1960, 62, 127–139); R. M. Jurjevich, Normative data for the clinical and additional MMPI scales for a population of delinquent girls (1963, 69, 143–146); R. W. Olson, MMPI sex differences in narcotic addicts (1964, 71, 257–266). *Journal of Psychology*: D. J. Baer and J. F. Moynihan, Stepwise discriminant-function analysis of seminary-candidate MMPI scores (1964, 58, 413–419); G. M. Guthrie, Six MMPI diagnostic profile patterns (1950, 30, 317–323); W. Schofield, A study of medical students with the MMPI: II. Group and individual changes after two years (1953, 36, 137–141).

NATIONAL COUNCIL ON CRIME AND DELINQUENCY. *Journal of Research in Crime and Delinquency*: R. E. Warman and T. E. Hannum, MMPI pattern changes in female prisoners (1965, 2, 72–76).

Quarterly Journal of Studies on Alcohol: A. C. Rosen, A comparative study of alcoholic and psychiatric patients with the MMPI (1960, 21, 253–266).

Psychological Reports: F. B. Stone, V. N. Rowley, and J. C. MacQueen, Using the MMPI with adolescents who have somatic symptoms (1966, 18, 139–147).

SPRINGER-VERLAG. *Psychopharmacologia*: E. S. Sulzer, The effects of promazine on MMPI performance in the chronic psychiatric patient (1961, 2, 137–140).

STATE HOSPITALS PRESS. *Psychiatric Quarterly Supplement*: W. M. Swenson and B. P. Grimes, Characteristics of sex offenders admitted to a Minnesota state hospital for presentence psychiatric investigation (1958, 31, 110–123).

UNIVERSITY OF KENTUCKY PRESS. J. C. Ball, *Social deviancy and adolescent personality*, Lexington, 1962.

UNIVERSITY OF MINNESOTA PRESS. S. R. Hathaway and E. D. Monachesi (Eds.), *Analyzing and predicting juvenile delinquency with the MMPI*, Minneapolis, 1953; S. R. Hathaway and E. D. Monachesi, *Adolescent personality and behavior*, Minneapolis, 1963; G. S. Welsh and W. G. Dahlstrom (Eds.), *Basic readings on the MMPI in psychology and medicine*, Minneapolis, 1956.

R.I.L.

University of Pittsburgh
May 1968

Contents

Parents of Disturbed Children

Prisoners

Student and Occupational Groups

Race and Culture

Miscellaneous Groups

Conditions of Administration

A HANDBOOK OF MMPI GROUP PROFILES

Introduction

THIS handbook reports 297 mean MMPI profiles of a wide range of diagnostic and behavioral groups, together with relevant information about the background of each group and the manner of selection and testing. It is designed to serve as a source book of basic data which can be drawn upon for both research and clinical purposes.

The author's original reason for collecting the material was to improve his own clinical skill in using the MMPI. In this vein, one contribution of the handbook is to indicate behavioral and other characteristics that are reflected in MMPI scores with some degree of consistency and also to point up characteristics that have little or no effect on the scores. The group profiles are not particularly well suited to be of direct aid in the interpretation of individual profiles; they are better regarded as a general source of information about the relationship of the MMPI to the diagnostic and behavioral categories represented. Thus, the most useful information for improving diagnostic skill can probably be gained by noting differences among the mean profiles of different diagnostic groups, rather than by attempting to find the group providing the best fit for an individual profile.

Use of the handbook as a source of research data needs little elaboration. It can be approached in two ways: as a source of test data about different groups of people or as a source of validity data about the MMPI. Either way, implications and suggestions for further research should be readily apparent.

Construction of the MMPI

Work on the MMPI was initiated in the late 1930's as the result of a perceived need in clinical research and practice for "an objective instrument for the multiphasic assessment of personality by means of a profile of scales" (Hathaway, 1960). Using an approach related to the empirical development of the Strong Vocational Interest Blank, Hathaway and McKinley (1940, 1951) built scales from the responses of patients who were classified according to the current clinical practice — at that time

based on a modified Kraepelinian system. The authors saw several potential advantages in the MMPI. It would be more convenient for the psychiatrist and clinical psychologist to use than a battery of independent scales prepared for special purposes: this one test would yield a comprehensive sampling of significant behavior. It could be used with persons of limited intelligence and education since the wording and manner of presentation were simpler than in the instruments which were then current. It would provide a large pool of items from which scales supplementing the original nine clinical and three validity scales might be constructed to meet special needs. For a more complete account of the place of the MMPI within the field of personality assessment in general, the reader is referred to the forthcoming text by Lanyon and Goodstein (*The Assessm_ t of Personality*, to be published by Wiley).

In the preliminary work more than one thousand statements were compiled from psychiatric examination forms, psychiatry textbooks, and previously published attitude and personality scales, as well as from the authors' clinical experience. Statements were written in a first-person self-report format. The list was refined to 504 items, which were printed on individual cards to be sorted by the patients as "true," "false," or "cannot say." In its latest form, the MMPI contains 550 different items, and is administered in the card format or from a printed booklet with a separate answer sheet. In the booklet, 16 items are repeated for ease of machine scoring. A tape-recorded form is also available.

Items for each scale of the MMPI were selected by contrasting the responses of nonpsychiatric subjects with those of patients in a particular diagnostic category. In these analyses more than 1500 nonpsychiatric subjects were used, of whom the main group comprised 724 visitors to the University of Minnesota Hospitals. Others were 265 normal clients from the University of Minnesota Testing Bureau, 265 local WPA workers, and 254 medical patients from the general wards of the University of

Minnesota Hospitals. Although all these subjects were available at one time or another, the original reports indicate that a group of about 600 was used in the preliminary item analyses.

More than 800 carefully studied psychiatric patients constituted the clinical pool. The individual criterion groups generally contained 50 or fewer subjects; in some cases more than one criterion group was utilized in an effort to improve the discriminating power of a scale. For example, more than a dozen scales were constructed in an unsuccessful attempt to obtain satisfactory discrimination among the subcategories of schizophrenia (Hathaway, 1956, p. 108). In addition, internal consistency analysis of preliminary items for a scale was sometimes performed. Usually several different combinations of items were proposed and each was tested by cross-validation. The usual method of item selection for a scale was as follows: A basic pool was assembled of items which showed a percentage frequency difference between the normal group and the criterion group of two or two and a half times the standard error. Items then were usually excluded if the frequency of response for both groups was very low or very high, if they failed to differentiate the criterion group from another of the normal groups which might be considered, or if the difference was obviously based on apparently irrelevant factors such as marital status. A good many items in the basic pool were also eliminated from each scale because they showed overlap in validity with some other clinical syndrome. However, no item was ever eliminated from a scale because its manifest content appeared unrelated to the syndrome in question.

Scoring

Raw scores on the basic clinical and validity scales are converted to standard or T scores (mean of 50, standard deviation of 10) by plotting them on a standardized profile form. The distributions are skewed in a positive direction, so that there are very few extremely low scores. For almost all normative groups except the original one, means of the scales tend to be a little higher than 50. This is possibly due to the fact that the original normative sample contained many of the subjects used in the normal criterion groups for scale construction. Preparation of a standard form early in the development of the MMPI was fortunate in that it served to fix the order of presentation of the scales, thereby facilitating analysis of patterns or configurations of scores. Since the meaning of the scales has become broader, through clinical usage and research, than their definition by the original criterion groups, they have come to be known by abbreviations or simply by numbers.

The mechanics of scoring the MMPI answer sheet and drawing the profile are set forth in the *Manual* (Hathaway and McKinley, 1951). It is important to check the accuracy of these clerical procedures, doubly so if the profile is an unusual one. To aid in classifying profiles and interpreting patterns, a numerical coding system was developed to provide the important characteristics in an easily handled summary form (Dahlstrom and Welsh, 1960, p. 18). The scale numbers are arranged in descending order of scale magnitude, and each standard deviation (range of 10 T scores) is separated from the next by a different punctuation sign. Profiles can be reconstructed from their codes with some little loss of precision.

In interpretation, reference is often made to "high" or "elevated" scores. As a rough guide, these terms should be taken to refer to a T score of about 70 or above, although this will vary according to the population, as discussed later. A "low" score may be considered to refer to a T score of 40 or below. Reference may also be made to the "highest" or "peak" scale. This is a useful concept when dealing with patients, since the scale with the highest T score is the most likely to reflect significant information, even if the peak is not particularly high.

The Scales

In the following paragraphs, description of the original clinical concepts and criterion groups is provided, together with notes on the interpretation of the scales. For the former information, the author has drawn heavily upon a series of articles by the test authors (Hathaway, 1956; Hathaway and McKinley, 1942; McKinley and Hathaway, 1940, 1942, 1944). All these articles appear in *Basic Readings on the MMPI in Psychology and Medicine* (Welsh and Dahlstrom, 1956). The interpretive notes have been based largely on the following sources, to which the reader is referred for more extensive material: Dahlstrom and Welsh (1960), Drake and Oetting (1959), Gilberstadt and Duker (1965), Good and Brantner (1961), Hathaway and Meehl (1951), and Marks and Seeman (1963).

Cannot say score (?). The cannot say or ? score is simply the number of items not responded to as true or false. The more items that are omitted, the more distorted the profile will become, especially if the omissions tend to be in one particular area of personality. The examiner can easily discourage excessive omissions, and often does so in order to circumvent this difficulty. If such instructions are given, however, the scale cannot be interpreted for personality meaning. Apart from evasiveness, there are several possible reasons for high ? scores. At times, seriously depressed patients leave many questions unanswered, since the magnitude of the task overwhelms them. Omissions may also result from an inability to understand the questions, due to language difficulties or inadequate intelligence or education. An obsessive-compulsive or unduly ruminative person who finds great difficulty in reaching decisions may likewise achieve a high ? score, but experience suggests that patients who omit as many as 60 items are unlikely to be neurotic. A convenient way to handle the problem of omissions is initially to give the standard instructions, which permit omissions, and then to return the test to the subject if more than about 10 items have been omitted.

Lie scale (L). The L scale was intended to provide a basis for evaluating subjects' general frankness in responding to the test items. Fifteen items were selected to reflect behavior which is socially desirable but obviously unlikely. Subjects achieving high scores on this scale have probably engaged in rather naive distortion in their responses to the remainder of the test.

The norms given for the L scale were set too low. The 70 T-score level should be represented by a raw score of 7, rather than 10 as the profile sheet suggests. The mean for normals is about 4. Since the items are psychologically rather obvious, high scorers are often people who have made a naive attempt to present themselves in a favorable light. Such people often tend to come from the lower socioeconomic levels or to have limited intelligence. Patients with high L scores tend to score somewhat lower than expected on the clinical scales, suggesting that these people are repressing or denying unfavorable characteristics throughout the test. High L scores may also be obtained by subjects who have a naive but genuine belief in their own virtues. Such people tend to be somewhat conventional and rigid in nature, and to lack insight into their own motivations.

Infrequency scale (F). The F scale contains 64 items which were endorsed by very few of the normal criterion subjects — usually less than 10 per cent. Although this is one of the longest scales of the test, normal subjects endorse a mean of about four items.

The norms given for the F scale were set too high. The 70 T-score level should be represented by a raw score of 16, rather than 13 as indicated on the profile sheet. Essentially, a high F score indicates an atypical or deviant set of responses. There are a number of purely technical reasons for such an occurrence: random responding by the subject, inadequate intelligence or education, lack of familiarity with the English language, inadequate vision, or a clerical error in scoring. These possibilities, which are usually responsible for a raw score greater than 16, should always be considered first. A second kind of reason for a high F score is a deliberate effort by the subject to present himself in an unfavorable light, or to convey the impression that he is emotionally disturbed. It is often difficult to distinguish between a person whose high F score represents simple malingering and a patient who is in fact disturbed but is exaggerating his disturbance as a "cry for help." The third reason for a high F score is that the deviance reflected in the score is representative of deviance in the subject. Thus, the F score is one general indicator of the amount of psychopathology a patient possesses. Nonconforming behavior in normal subjects is reflected by a slightly elevated F score.

Correction scale (K). The K scale was derived after the original development of the test as a correction scale or "suppressor variable" for improving the discriminations of the clinical scales, by taking into consideration different degrees of test-taking defensiveness or frankness. Most of the items were selected by comparing the responses of normal subjects with those of 50 psychiatric patients who obtained high scores on the L scale and whose clinical scores were in the normal range; that is, patients whose scores suggested excessive defensiveness. Eight items were included in the K scale to counteract the tendency of certain patient groups to score excessively low on an earlier version of the scale without apparent psychological justification for doing so. Various fractions of the K score are added to the raw scores for several of the clinical scales to improve their discrimination. The authors recognized that the K weights given in the *Manual* might not be optimal for populations other than their own, and subsequent work (e.g., Heilbrun, 1963) has tended to substantiate this prediction. However, the vast majority of research and clinical data available on the MMPI refer to the K-corrected form using the original K weights.

Although the primary function of the K scale is to increase the discriminating power of the clinical scales, it can be interpreted in its own right as a validity scale and also as a personality scale. The K score may be considered to reflect test-taking attitudes of a more subtle nature than the L scale. A K raw score of 25 or more indicates rather extreme claims of freedom from personal defects; such a score signals that caution should be used in making further interpretation of the profile. A low K score may result from frankness and willingness to reveal weaknesses. An extremely low score suggests a lack of adequate defenses and perhaps a tendency toward exaggeration of symptoms in the "cry for help" manner of some high F scorers. The F minus K difference has in fact been suggested as an index of exaggeration in a pathological direction (Gough, 1950). College students and subjects of higher socioeconomic and educational levels tend to score higher than other groups on the K scale, so that an elevated K score for such people does not have the same implications as it does for those of lower socioeconomic and educational status. A moderate elevation in normal subjects, especially of the former kind, can suggest insight, self-satisfaction, and psychological sophistication.

General comments on the validity scales. Examination of the validity scales ?, L, F, and K is usually the first step in the interpretation of an MMPI profile. These scales tend to have two different kinds of meaning. First, they allow an evaluation of the general validity of the profile and the confidence which can be placed in it; e.g., whether the subject adequately understood the items, whether he tried to present himself in an unduly favorable or unduly poor light, or whether he was too disturbed to cooperate adequately. Second, these scales, like the clinical scales, are related to personality and other characteristics. As would be expected from the individual descriptions above, psychiatric patients typically show an inverted "V" pattern for the L, F, and K scales, indicating the presence of psychological deviance together with recognition of this state. The upright "V" pattern is shown by a few defensive patients who tend not to give significant elevations on the clinical scales, and by neurotics who channel their psychological difficulties through some kind of physical complaint.

Scale 1: Hypochondriasis (Hs). Hypochondriasis was defined as "abnormal psychoneurotic concern over bodily health." Fifty cases of "relatively pure, uncomplicated hypochondriasis" were selected. Great care was exercised to exclude patients showing indications of psychosis. To assure that the final scale did not merely reflect general emotional maladjustment, use was also made of 50 nonhypochondriacal patients who showed high scores on a preliminary version of the scale.

High scorers on the Hs scale are unduly concerned about their physical health, tending to claim symptoms for which no clear organic basis can be found, and to exaggerate the importance of any organic malfunctioning which they do have. Although persons with real physical illnesses may obtain slightly elevated scores, a T score of 65 or more usually suggests some psychological involvement. When the highest scores for a patient occur on the Hs and Hy scales, the likelihood of psychophysiological complaints is high. This MMPI pattern is very common in a psychiatric population, usually indicating a neurotic disorder. It is more usual in women than in men, and suggests passivity.

Scale 2: Depression (D). This scale was developed to measure symptomatic depression, the authors' term for patients showing "a clinically recognizable, general frame of mind characterized by poor morale, lack of hope in the future, and dissatisfaction with the patient's own status generally." The criterion group contained 50 patients, most of whom were in the depressed phase of a manic-depressive psychosis. Testing was done as close to the time of diagnosis of depression as possible. As far as could be determined, they represented relatively "pure" cases of depression. In constructing the scale, use was also made of the responses of 40 normal persons having a high score on a preliminary depression scale, and 50 patients who appeared not to be depressed but who also scored high on the preliminary scale.

This scale is the most frequent high point among psychiatric patients, a fact that is not surprising since it was designed to reflect unhappiness and poor morale. It is considered to be fairly sensitive to fluctuations in mood. High scorers are readily aware of their proneness toward excessive worry and pessimism, and it is likely that a moderate elevation on the D scale is a favorable prognostic sign, since such persons are motivated to make changes. It is sometimes suggested that patients who score high on the D scale but deny depressive feelings and in fact do not show depressive behavior should be watched carefully for possible suicidal intent. Peak scores on the D and Pt scales are fairly common, suggesting neurosis with depression and anxiety.

Scale 3: Hysteria (Hy). The Hy scale was intended as an aid in the clinical diagnosis of hysteria. The criterion patients either had been diagnosed "psychoneurosis, hysteria," or had been observed to have hysterical components in their disturbance. In some cases a doubt remained about the presence of a true organic illness or early schizophrenia. Several tentative criterion groups were identified; the final group contained 50 patients.

High scores on the Hy scale are fairly common for women but rather infrequent for men. An elevated score suggests a tendency toward some particular somatic complaint or symptom, particularly when under psychological stress, with a simultaneous tendency to claim superior social adjustment. Patients with high scores on the Hy scale often show accompanying elevations on the Hs and D scales, indicating a mixed neurotic disorder. The inverted "V" pattern, mentioned above, has been interpreted as suggesting the clinical *belle indifférence* of the hysteric, with the lower score on the D scale reflecting the lack of concern over the physical complaints indicated by the higher Hs and Hy scales. Among normals, high scores on the Hy scale suggest sociability and enthusiasm, perhaps accompanied by a certain amount of immaturity, suggestibility, and egocentrism.

Scale 4: Psychopathic deviate (Pd). The basic clinical group consisted of 100 persons who appeared to fit the asocial type of psychopathic personality as described in the psychiatric literature. The criterion patients were those diagnosed psychopathic personality, asocial and amoral type. Those with psychotic or neurotic manifestations were eliminated. Most of the patients were in the age range 17–22, and their histories were characterized by behavior such as stealing, lying, truancy, sexual promiscuity, alcoholic overindulgence, and forgery. All had long histories of minor delinquency, and their behavior was poorly motivated and poorly concealed. There were more females than males. Use was made of two further groups: 78 additional psychiatric patients who satisfied the criterion, and 100 male prisoners at a federal reformatory.

Elevations on the Pd scale suggest nonconformity and a rejection of normal social conventions. Prison and de-

linquent groups, as expected from the derivation of the scale, show marked elevations. Peak scores on the Pd scale can often be interpreted similarly. Adolescents in general tend to score slightly higher than older persons. The scale was developed to reflect the concept of "psychopathic deviancy," which refers to people who are unable to form satisfactory emotional relationships or to appreciate the feelings of others and who cannot anticipate the consequences of their own behavior. They continually engage in antisocial and self-defeating behavior in spite of adequate intelligence and opportunity. Peaks on the D and Pd scales (or D, Pd, and Pt), suggesting a passive aggressive personality pattern, are not uncommon among alcoholics and drug addicts.

Scale 5: Masculinity-femininity (Mf). The definition of this concept posed problems which were not satisfactorily resolved. The main criterion group consisted of 13 homosexual invert males, whose responses were contrasted with those of normal males. Use was also made of a group of feminine males identified by another inventory, and of differences in frequency of response to items by normal males and females.

High scores on the Mf scale are designed to indicate feminine interests in men and masculine interests in women. Although homosexual men tend to show high scores, so do other groups, in particular those with artistic or literary interests. College males tend to score slightly higher than the normative group. Higher scores in men indicate emotional sensitivity, cultural interests, and perhaps some degree of passivity, as opposed to the more mechanical, scientific, outdoor, and athletic interests of lower scorers. To some extent the reverse descriptions are true for women. Low-scoring women often demonstrate a strong feminine interest pattern.

Scale 6: Paranoia (Pa). The criterion patients were those judged to have paranoid symptoms, although the diagnostic label of paranoia was rarely applied. More often they were diagnosed paranoid state, paranoid condition, and paranoid schizophrenia. Their symptoms included ideas of reference, feelings of persecution, and grandiose self-concepts; or, more mildly, suspiciousness, rigidity, and excessive personal sensitivity.

The Pa scale is considered to be fairly weak; many items are obvious in content and express socially undesirable thoughts and actions. Although high scores suggest suspiciousness, fixed beliefs, and perhaps formal paranoid signs, the majority of paranoid patients do not achieve particularly high scores. Moderate scores often indicate excessive interpersonal sensitivity, secretiveness, and a tendency to blame others for one's misfortunes.

Scale 7: Psychasthenia (Pt). The term psychasthenia, now obsolete, was applied to individuals with compulsions, obsessions, unreasonable fears, and excessive doubts. While such symptoms are not uncommon in the general population, they are so strong and numerous in some people as to interfere considerably with social or vocational adjustment. Since these people are usually seen by lay counselors or in outpatient services, some difficulty was encountered in forming an adequate criterion group. The final group contained 20 patients who had been studied intensively both medically and psychiatrically. Items were added to the preliminary scale on the basis of correlations of items with the scores on the preliminary scale.

The Pt scale is perhaps the best single MMPI indicator of general anxiety. High scorers tend to suffer from excessive doubts, to ruminate at length, and to have pervasive feelings of guilt and insecurity. Many such persons are compulsively introspective, and ruminate endlessly to no effect. This scale is strongly related to the Sc scale, and an elevation on Pt often accompanies high scores on the "neurotic" scales Hs, D, and Hy. Patients with peaks on scales Hs, Hy, and Pt are often phobic about physical illness.

Scale 8: Schizophrenia (Sc). Criterion patients for this scale were those diagnosed to have schizophrenia in one or another of its various subtypes. There were two partly overlapping criterion groups of 50 patients, of whom more were males than females. The final scale was one of a large number of preliminary scales, which included more than a dozen subscales derived from the four subclassifications of schizophrenia: catatonic, paranoid, simple, and hebephrenic.

The Sc scale is also relatively weak. Many schizophrenics do not score high on the scale, although there is evidence that most persons with a T score of 75 or above show some schizoid thinking. Agitated neurotic patients may also score high on this scale. High scorers in the normal population often tend to be somewhat emotionally isolated, nonconforming, and withdrawn, with many anxieties and internal conflicts. However, the vast majority are able to maintain adequate social adjustment in spite of their conflicts and difficulties, so that the label "schizophrenic" should be used with great circumspec-

tion. Among patients, peaks on the Pa and Sc scales often suggest paranoid schizophrenia. Scales Pt and Sc are highly correlated, suggesting a similarity between the underlying concepts. Peaks on the scales D, Pt, and Sc are quite common among schizophrenics, but also suggest an acute anxiety reaction.

Scale 9: Hypomania (Ma). The term hypomania was employed to describe the milder degrees of manic excitement typically occurring in manic-depressive psychosis. Hypomanic trends tend to follow the cardinal symptoms of the manic condition (elated but unstable mood, psychomotor excitement, and flight of ideas), but are often relatively unobtrusive. The criterion group contained 24 patients. Their degree of mania was necessarily not more than moderate, since the more severe patients would not cooperate adequately in testing. Patients with delirium, confusional states, signs of other psychoses, or agitated depressions were excluded.

High-scoring patients on the Ma scale are hyperactive, impulsive, and unpredictable, elated but unstable in mood, restless, overoptimistic, and easily distractible. Moderate elevations on this scale in both patients and normals suggest milder degrees of these characteristics. Patients with peaks on the D and Ma scales are not uncommon, and a sizable minority of them are suffering from brain damage. Peaks on scales Hs and Ma or Hs, Hy, and Ma are also at times associated with brain damage. Peaks on scales Pd and Ma, or Pd, Sc, and Ma, are relatively common among prisoners and juvenile delinquents, suggesting inadequate controls over antisocial and hostile tendencies, with consequent impulsive acting-out behavior. The prognosis for such persons in psychodynamic therapy is considered to be poor. Patients with peaks on the Sc and Ma scales often are agitated schizophrenics.

Scale 0: Social introversion (Si). Although not one of the original clinical scales, the Si scale (Drake, 1946) appears on the MMPI profile form and is widely used. Items were selected from among those which differentiated two groups of female students at the University of Wisconsin: 50 high scorers and 50 low scorers on the social introversion-extroversion scale of the Minnesota T-S-E inventory. Cross-validity was demonstrated for male students.

High scorers on the Si scale tend to be introverted, shy, and socially inept, and prefer to avoid social activity. Low scorers are gregarious, outgoing, sociable, enthusiastic, assertive, talkative, and adept at interpersonal manipulation.

ADDITIONAL SCALES

The authors' hope that additional scales would be constructed has been fully realized. A total of 213 scales, indexes, and special scoring procedures are listed by Dahlstrom and Welsh (1960). Many of these additional scales are subsets of the items in one of the original scales, grouped according to rational considerations (e.g., Harris and Lingoes, 1955), factorial purity (e.g., Comrey, 1957), or uniqueness of the items (e.g., Welsh, 1952). Most of the other scales were empirically derived in the manner of the original scales and were intended to identify members of other diagnostic or behavioral groups. In general, construction of these scales has been somewhat less painstaking than the original scale development, with the result that relatively few of the newer scales have achieved more than sporadic popularity. The following are perhaps the most widely used.

Factor scales A and R. It has been demonstrated through factor analytic procedures that many of the MMPI items can be assigned to one of two general categories or factors. Scales A and R were constructed by Welsh (1956) to assess these two main factors. Scale A appears to reflect anxiety or general emotional upset, and scale R has been considered related to the concepts of repression and introversion.

Ego strength scale (Es). Developed by Barron (1953a), the Es scale consists of items which discriminated 17 neurotic patients who were judged to have improved after six months of individual psychotherapy from 16 patients who were judged unimproved. Although the criterion groups were small, subsequent evidence has shown the scale to be valid in other psychotherapy settings.

Manifest anxiety scale (At). The At scale was originally developed by Taylor (1953) for use in basic research on Hullian drive theory. Items included were those four out of five judges agreed upon as related to anxiety. There is research evidence for the validity of the scale, which tends to correlate highly with the Pt and Sc scales.

The Group Profiles

The group profiles collected here lend support to a broad generalization often made by MMPI users, namely, that the three traditional psychiatric groupings — psychosis, neurosis, and personality disorder — tend to show distinctive MMPI patterns. With some exceptions, the D, Pd, Pa, and Sc scales (2, 4, 6, and 8) represent the highest scores for the schizophrenic and other psychotic groups; the neurotic groups tend to score highest on scales Hs, D, Hy, and Pt (1, 2, 3, and 7); and the personality disorder, prisoner, and delinquent groups tend to have their highest scores on the Pd, Sc, and Ma scales (4, 8, and 9).

It is not the author's intention to catalog all the MMPI differences among the groups represented in this book. However, the effects of certain demographic and other variables, an understanding of which is basic to the use of the instrument, are summarized below. General comments on interpretation will follow, and then a description of the pattern followed in presentation of the group profiles here.

DEMOGRAPHIC AND OTHER VARIABLES

Age. Age differences account for several distinct though minor variations in MMPI profiles. First, normal adolescents tend to score slightly higher than average on the Pd scale and also on Sc and Ma. Second, the scores of elderly subjects show a slight increase on the Hs and Si scales. Third, the data of one study suggest that the scores of schizophrenic patients tend to decrease with age, although this finding is not entirely consistent with indirect comparisons which can be made among different studies.

Sex. As has been previously suggested (e.g., Marks and Seeman, 1963), sex appears to make little consistent difference in the MMPI scores of behavioral and diagnostic groups. One exception is the Mf scale, on which female psychiatric groups tend to score slightly lower than males.

Race and culture. Group profiles of Negro and white normal subjects are similar except for slightly higher scores among the male Negro groups on the L and Ma scales. Scores for students in another English-speaking culture (Australia) appear fairly similar to those of United States students. However, preliminary efforts at translation of the MMPI into other languages (Italian and German) produced wide differences with comparison groups from the United States, and scores for subjects responding to foreign-language versions cannot be considered comparable to scores for English-speaking subjects in the forms reported.

Socioeconomic status and education. There seem to be no consistent differences due to socioeconomic status, although the relevant data are scanty. With regard to education, highly educated males score consistently higher than average on the Mf scale. Male college groups typically show a slight elevation on both the Mf and the Ma scales. Limited education appears not to make a consistent difference on any scale, though once again the relevant data are sparse.

Form of administration. No differences of any practical significance have been reported between the booklet and card or the booklet and oral (tape-recorded) forms of the MMPI.

Test-retest. If original and retest profiles are compared, small but definite differences appear. Scores on the K scale tend to be higher on retest, while the clinical scales are slightly lower. These differences do not seem to be of any great practical significance.

INDIVIDUAL INTERPRETATION

Although not well suited for this purpose, the group profiles can be employed directly as a guide to individual interpretation if certain cautions and limitations are kept in mind. It is important to remember that the profiles represent *mean* scores of diagnostic and behavioral groups and thus can be regarded only as demonstrating *trends* within the groups. Individual members of a group will of course vary widely, so that even approximate conformity to the group profile will be the exception rather than the rule.

The standard deviation of scale scores among normal subjects was fixed at 10, although among psychiatric groups it may be as large as 16 or 18, and occasionally more for scales with high mean scores. Thus, it would be foolish to try to diagnose, for example, the presence of brain damage in a patient from a comparison of his MMPI profile with the relevant group profiles, or to attempt to delineate individuals who are good or poor drivers on this basis. However, for characteristics which are more specifically reflected in the MMPI, such as personality disorder, useful information can often be gained about an individual profile by exclusion. For example, if an individual profile is found to be 20 or more points lower than relevant normative groups for personality disorder on several scales, including the critical scales Pd and Ma, then this particular diagnostic category could be ruled out with some degree of confidence.

A further point to be noted is that the group profiles in this handbook are not comparable with those presented by Gilberstadt and Duker (1965) or by Marks and Seeman (1963) in their interpretive manuals. These latter profiles are the mean scores of *subjects chosen on the basis of MMPI criteria*, rather than subjects grouped according to diagnostic labels or behavioral characteristics. Mean profiles in the other manuals will tend to have higher scores and smaller standard deviations than those in the present volume.

IMPORTANCE OF BASE RATES

Users of the MMPI and similar instruments often fail to realize that the interpretation to be placed on a high score varies according to the nature of the group of which the subject is a member. For example, a high score on the Sc scale for a patient in a psychiatric hospital has an entirely different meaning from a similar score obtained by a college student tested for research purposes.

Let us see why this is so. Hathaway (1956) reported that on the K-corrected Sc scale about 60 per cent of schizophrenic patients in the psychiatric cross-validation group achieved a T score of 70 or greater, whereas only 2 per cent of the normal cross-validation subjects scored in this range. Suppose the scale is used for diagnosis in a clinic where approximately half the patients are schizophrenic and the other half are "normal." Simple calculation (Meehl and Rosen, 1955) will show that calling schizophrenic all patients who score 70 or more will result in 79 per cent of all patients being correctly diagnosed. The calculation is shown in Table 1. Further, of those patients diagnosed schizophrenic by the test, 30/31 or 97 per cent are in fact schizophrenic. Most of the errors made will be in the direction of mislabeling schizophrenics as nonschizophrenic, so that a *lower* cutting score (e.g., 65) would raise the over-all diagnostic efficiency. The main point is that the use of 70 as a cutting

Table 1. Percentage of Patients Diagnosed Schizophrenic or Normal by the Sc Scale, Using a Cutoff Score of 70, Where 50 Per Cent Are Actually Schizophrenic and 50 Per Cent Are Actually Normal

T Score	Actually Schizo-phrenic	Actually Normal	Total
70 or more (diagnosed schizophrenic)	30*	1	31
Below 70 (diagnosed normal)	20	49*	69
Total	50	50	100

* Correctly diagnosed.

score assures that almost all patients labeled schizophrenic by the test are in fact schizophrenic. It should be pointed out that the Sc scale is in practice not quite so successful as portrayed here, because some of the 50 per cent called normal will achieve high Sc scores owing to other disorders.

Now suppose we were to give the test to apparently normal college students. Let us assume that about 1 per cent of these students are schizophrenic. If the same cutting score of 70 is used, the test will diagnose *2.6* per cent of them as schizophrenics. This situation is represented in Table 2. In other words, most of the students scoring

Table 2. Percentage of Students Diagnosed Schizophrenic or Normal by the Sc Scale Using a Cutoff Score of 70, Where 1 Per Cent Are Actually Schizophrenic and 99 Per Cent Are Actually Normal

T Score	Actually Schizophrenic	Actually Normal	Total
70 or more (diagnosed schizophrenic)	0.6	2.0	2.6
Below 70 (diagnosed normal)	0.4	97.0	97.4
Total	1.0	99.0	100.0

70 or more on the Sc scale are *not schizophrenic*. However, it is reasonable to believe that they would tend to be different in some way or other from the lower scoring students, and research has shown this to be true. In other words, high scores in a normal population are generally to be interpreted within the range of normal personality functioning. Interpretations of a psychiatric nature can be made on very high scores or on profile patterns that research has shown to signify pathology in such a group. In the interpretive notes earlier in this Introduction, only sporadic references were made to differences in interpretation for normal subjects and psychiatric patients, and most of the material was oriented toward psychiatric patients. However, the examples above should make it clear that the degree of abnormality to be assigned in the interpretation of any profile will depend in the first instance on the likelihood of pathology occurring in the population of which the subject is a member. It should also be recognized that when a student seeks help in a university counseling service, he becomes a member of the population of help-seekers, in which the likelihood of pathology is greater than among students not seeking help. Thus, the interpretation of his MMPI would change accordingly.

As a general rule, with any characteristic whose presence in a population is infrequent, such as schizophrenia in a normal population, or cerebral disease among psychiatric outpatients, the probability of successfully employing the MMPI to identify persons possessing it is small (Meehl and Rosen, 1955). In these instances, identification can only be made satisfactorily from some sign whose predictive power for the disorder in question is very high, such as the discovery of a brain lesion or a history of previous schizophrenic episodes.

ARRANGEMENT OF THE GROUP PROFILES

The profiles in this volume are divided into 13 categories. The headings of the first six categories follow the American Psychiatric Association's *Diagnostic and Statistical Manual* (American Psychiatric Association, 1952), while the remainder have been chosen for convenience of reference. Abnormal groups tend to come toward the beginning; normal groups toward the end. Profiles that could have been put into more than one category have been placed in accordance with the major intention of the original research. Occasionally a profile is repeated for purposes of comparison. Arrangement of the profiles within each of the 13 categories is for convenience of reference. The number of profiles drawn on each grid has been limited to two for ease in reading.

The following guidelines were employed as an aid in selecting the groups reported: (a) each group possessed some noteworthy behavioral or biographical characteristic, defined independently of the MMPI itself; (b) at least a minimal amount of descriptive information was available about the group; and (c) groups showing few or no distinctive MMPI characteristics were included in order to indicate behaviors that are *not* reflected in the MMPI. Although groups were excluded for a number of minor reasons, the general policy was to include all available data meeting the minimum requirements. It is hoped that in any future revision of this volume, a more selective policy can be followed as additional studies become available. It should be evident that in the present collection certain areas tend to be overrepresented while others are incomplete.

With each profile is an abstract reporting all the information considered relevant to understanding the profile that was given at its source. Initially an attempt was made to write the authors for any basic information (such as mean age) that was missing from the original report, but this practice was discontinued after it was found that such information was seldom available if not originally presented. Although the abstracts vary widely in degree of completeness, the available information is arranged, with minor exceptions, in the format described below.

For convenience of reference, a number has been assigned to each "study" (some of the abstracts, of course, report only part of the original study), along with a descriptive title. The first paragraph of each abstract gives the geographic location and general nature of the groups (e.g., VA mental hygiene clinic patients), together with any information about the method of selection or testing that is common to all groups. Demographic data have been reported here if they were available only for several groups collectively. Also reported here is information on the use of the validity scales ?, L, F, and K. In some groups, individuals were systematically rejected on the basis of high validity scores, while others included all subjects regardless of validity indications. Further, the rules for exclusion varied and were often not stated in the original reports. This has necessarily resulted in some inconsistency in the present handbook, and readers are warned that over-all elevations of profiles from different studies are not always comparable.

In the second paragraph of the abstract (or the first, if collective description is not appropriate) are found specific identifying characteristics of each group represented and any further general information that logically belongs after rather than before the descriptions of the individual groups.

Where available, statistical comparisons between groups are given in a concluding paragraph of the abstract. Differences beyond the 5 per cent level of significance have been noted whenever they were reported. If the original study examined for significant differences but failed to find any, that has also been noted. If statistical comparisons were not mentioned in the original report, no mention of them is made in the abstract. In some cases, additional MMPI scores were available besides the 13 scales shown on the profiles. Significant differences on three of these additional scales (Barron's Es scale, and Welsh's A and R scales) have been included.

The figures showing the group profiles are keyed to the abstracts by use of the study number — followed by a, b, etc., if there is more than one figure accompanying the abstract. The caption for each figure includes the following information: the name of each group (the labels used in the original reports have been employed as far as possible, though some changes have been made for purposes of uniformity); sex and size of each group; the mean (or median) and range for age, intelligence, and years of education, when available for each group separately.

To provide a uniform presentation, all profiles have been K-corrected, except where scores on the K scale were not reported. K-uncorrected profiles are specifically identified as such. It is recognized that the value of K corrections is somewhat in doubt, and that ideally they should be determined afresh for each specific population. However, general usage has been followed in employing the K-correction weights offered in the 1951 *Manual* and on the regular profile blank.

THE GROUP PROFILES

Psychotic Disorders

Study 1: ACUTE AND CHRONIC PSYCHOSIS (Silver and Sines, 1961). *See Figures 1a–1d.*

The subjects were drawn from the Fergus Falls (Minnesota) State Hospital population. All patients tested were included in the study, regardless of validity scale values.

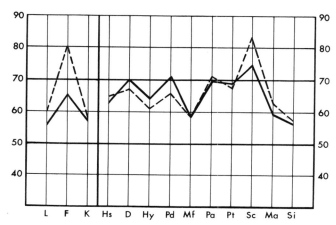

Figure 1a. Acute and Chronic Schizophrenia (Male). *Solid Line*: Acute Schizophrenics (N=67, Mean Age approx. 40, Age Range 14–63). *Broken Line*: Chronic Schizophrenics (N=164, Mean Age approx. 49, Age Range 18–76).

All literate, testable, newly admitted patients under age 65 completed the MMPI within five days following admission to the hospital as part of a routine psychological test battery. Those whose subsequent psychiatric diagnosis was schizophrenia or affective psychosis formed the acute psychosis groups. Diagnosis may have been influenced by the patient's MMPI characteristics. All patients on the continued treatment wards, exclusive of geriatric and medical units, who passed an initial screening test for reading and demonstrated ability to comprehend the directions also were given the MMPI. About half the patients on these wards completed the test. Those whose psychiatric diagnosis was schizophrenia or affective psychosis formed the chronic psychosis groups. The diagnosis of the chronic patients was largely uninfluenced by the MMPI.

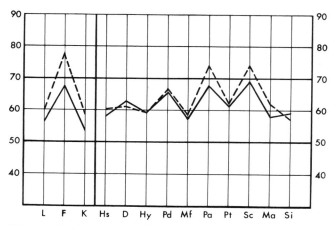

Figure 1b. Acute and Chronic Schizophrenia (Female). *Solid Line*: Acute Schizophrenics (N=97, Mean Age approx. 39, Age Range 13–64). *Broken Line*: Chronic Schizophrenics (N=133, Mean Age approx. 47, Age Range 19–78).

Comparison of the schizophrenia samples showed that the male acute group scored higher than the male chronic group on the Pd scale, and lower on the F and Sc scales; and the female acute group scored lower than the female chronic group on the F, K, Pa, Sc, and Es scales. Comparison of the affective psychosis samples showed that the male acute group scored higher than the male chronic

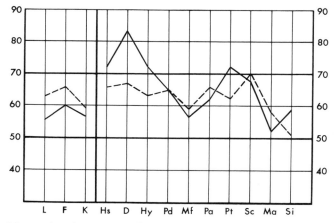

Figure 1c. Acute and Chronic Affective Psychosis (Male). *Solid Line*: Acute Affective Psychotics (N=28). *Broken Line*: Chronic Affective Psychotics (N=20).

15

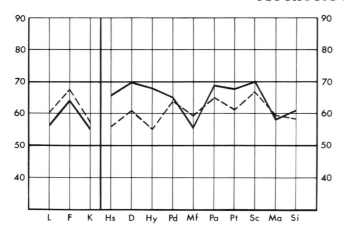

Figure 1d. Acute and Chronic Affective Psychosis (Female). *Solid Line*: Acute Affective Psychotics (N=48). *Broken Line*: Chronic Affective Psychotics (N=29).

group on the D, Hy, Pt, and Si scales; and the female acute group scored higher than the female chronic group on the Hs, D, Hy, and Pt scales, and lower on the Es scale.

Additional comparisons are reported in the original article.

Study 2: PARANOID SCHIZOPHRENIA (Rosen, 1958). *See Figure 2.*

The subjects were white veterans from the psychiatry service of the Minneapolis VA Hospital who had been diagnosed according to the VA psychiatric nomenclature as schizophrenic reaction, paranoid type. All subjects had been tested within 15 days of admission and before any physical treatment.

Comparison of the group with four neurotic samples

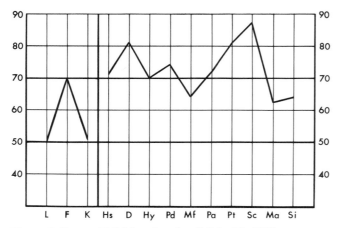

Figure 2. Paranoid Schizophrenics (Male, N=100).

(see Study 15) showed that the paranoid schizophrenics scored higher than each of these four groups on the F, Pd, Pa, Sc, and Ma scales, and higher than three of the groups on the Mf and Pt scales.

Study 3: PARANOID SCHIZOPHRENIA AND MANIC CONDITION (Guthrie, 1950). *See Figure 3.*

The subjects were patients in a mental hospital and in a veterans' hospital in Ontario, Canada. Only those patients on whom there was complete agreement among the psychiatric staff regarding diagnosis were included.

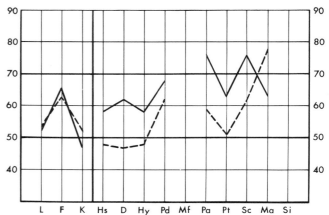

Figure 3. Paranoid Schizophrenia and Manic Condition (Male and Female). *Solid Line*: Paranoid Schizophrenics (N=25). *Broken Line*: Manics (N=11).

The influence of the psychometric findings on the diagnosis was minimal since the diagnosis of the psychiatrist was recorded before the psychometric findings were presented.

Only those patients showing strong evidence of hallucinations and/or delusions as well as other schizophrenic features were included in the paranoid schizophrenia group. Nine of the patients in the manic condition group were diagnosed manic depressive—manic phase, and the remaining two were diagnosed hypomanic.

Study 4: SCHIZOPHRENIA (Eichman, 1959). *See Figure 4.*

The subjects consisted of all the female veterans in the VA Hospital, Roanoke, Virginia, who had been administered the MMPI and who had received the diagnoses described below. Approximately half had taken the test on admission as part of a battery, and the test re-

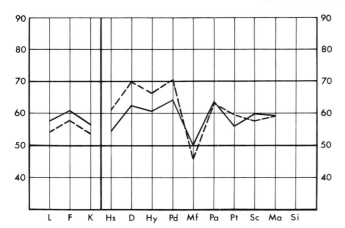

Figure 4. Schizophrenia (Female). *Solid Line*: Schizophrenics (N=56, Mean Age 34). *Broken Line*: Nonschizophrenics (N=33, Mean Age 37).

sults had had some influence on diagnosis. The remaining half had taken the test for different purposes, such as pre-psychotherapy evaluation or evaluation of current status, and the test had had no influence on diagnosis.

Those in the schizophrenia group had received one of the following diagnoses: chronic undifferentiated (29), paranoid (20), catatonic (2), schizo-affective (2), hebephrenic (2), and simple (1). Those in the nonschizophrenic control group had received a diagnosis of neurosis (20) or character or personality disorder (13).

Study 5: SCHIZOPHRENIA (Taulbee and Sisson, 1957). *See Figure 5.*

The subjects were 50 VA patients and 30 patients from a state hospital. The extent to which the MMPI contributed to the diagnosis is not known, but it is be-

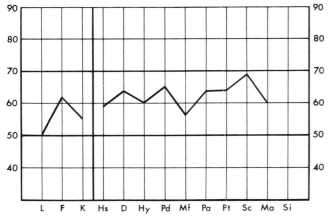

Figure 5. Schizophrenics (Male, N=80).

lieved that in the majority of cases the diagnoses were minimally influenced by the MMPI findings.

Comparison with a group of inpatient neurotics from the same VA hospital (see Study 13) showed that the schizophrenics scored higher on the F, Pa, Sc, and Ma scales, and lower on the Hs, D, and Hy scales.

Study 6: SCHIZOPHRENIA AT DIFFERENT AGES (Wauck, 1950). *See Figures 6a–6b.*

The subjects were clinically diagnosed schizophrenic patients at the Chicago State Hospital. There were 37 males and 43 females. Subclassification was as follows: paranoid 31; mixed 17; undetermined 22; simple 4; with manic features 2; catatonic 2; in psychopathic personality 1; and hebephrenic 1. The individual form of the

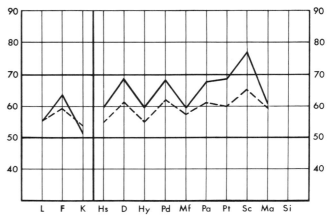

Figure 6a. Schizophrenia at Ages 15–29 and 30–39 (Male and Female). *Solid Line*: Age Group 15–29 (N=33). *Broken Line*: Age Group 30–39 (N=31).

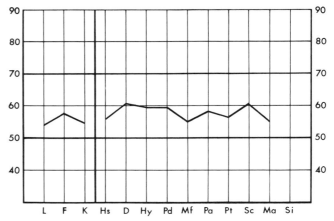

Figure 6b. Schizophrenia Age Group 40–53 (Male and Female, N=16).

17

MMPI was used, and this meant there was a selection factor since only those patients who could read and co-operate sufficiently well were tested.

The sample was divided into three age levels: 15–29, 30–39, and 40–53.

Study 7: SUBCLINICAL SCHIZOPHRENIA (Peterson, 1954a). *See Figure 7.*

The subjects were white veterans whose case records and MMPI profiles were on file at a VA mental hygiene clinic.

The subclinical schizophrenia sample was obtained by searching the complete file of the clinic for all patients who met the following criteria: (a) they were examined by a psychologist and were seen for at least two interviews by staff members at the clinic; (b) they received a diagnosis which contained no derivative of the word schizophrenia; and (c) they were later sent to a psychiatric hospital where they were said to be schizophrenic. The nonschizophrenic sample was obtained by examining the records of nonhospitalized patients at the clinic. Each "subclinical schizophrenic" was compared consec-

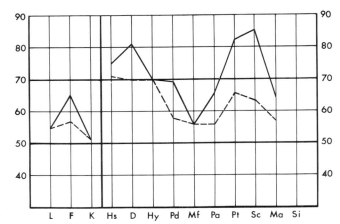

Figure 7. Subclinical Schizophrenia (Male). *Solid Line*: Subclinical Schizophrenics (N=33). *Broken Line*: Nonschizophrenics (N=33).

utively with patients listed in the nonhospitalized sample until one was found who had received an identical primary diagnosis. For these cases, neither diagnosis nor outpatient status was subsequently changed. The sample did not differ from the subclinical schizophrenia sample in age, education, or intelligence.

Psychoneurotic Disorders

Study 8: ANXIETY STATE AND INADEQUATE PERSONALITY (Guthrie, 1950). *See Figure 8.*

The subjects were patients in a mental hospital and a veterans' hospital in Ontario, Canada. Only those patients on whom there was complete agreement among the psychiatric staff regarding diagnosis were included. The influence of the psychometric findings on the diagnosis was minimal since the diagnosis of the psychiatrist was recorded before the psychometric findings were presented.

This anxiety state category included patients who complained of tenseness, worry, inability to sleep, and a variety of mild somatic complaints. Their final diagnosis, made at the time of discharge from the hospital, indicated that all were considered recovered or improved. In the category psychoneurosis, inadequate personality, were placed those neurotics who showed a long history of marginal adjustment, a low tolerance to anxiety, and

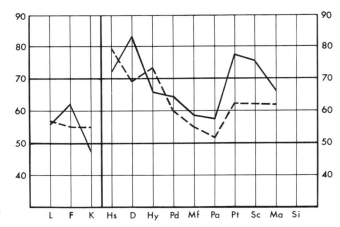

Figure 8. Anxiety State and Inadequate Personality (Male). *Solid Line*: Anxiety State Group (N=12). *Broken Line*: Inadequate Personality Group (N=19).

a poor response to treatment. There was usually a strong component of somatic complaints which could best be

18

described as neurasthenic. None of these patients had a history of delinquency.

Study 9: CONVERSION HYSTERIA (Fricke, 1956). *See Figure 9.*

The subjects were female patients who had been diagnosed conversion hysteria and tested with the MMPI since 1943 in the University of Minnesota Hospitals.

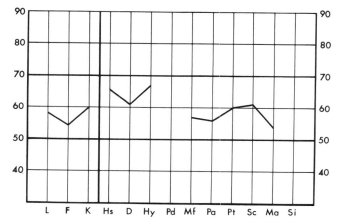

Figure 9. Conversion Hysteria Group (Female, N=63).

Cases with high L, F, or K scores were not discarded. Most patients were tested with the individual card form of the MMPI.

Study 10: NEUROSIS (Schofield, 1950). *See Figure 10.*

The subjects were patients from the Psychopathic Unit of the University of Minnesota Hospitals.

The outpatient group consisted of patients who had been briefly hospitalized (for an average of 6 days, range 2–18) before being discharged for treatment as outpatients. Diagnostic classification was psychoneurosis (22), simple schizophrenia (1), hypomania (1), and undiagnosed (1). Sixty-three per cent had a high school education or better, and 32 per cent were single. No evaluation of improvement in these patients was available. The inpatient group consisted of patients who had been hospitalized and had subsequently been discharged as improved or recovered. The MMPI was obtained at admission. Diagnostic classification was psychoneurosis, mixed (13), hysteria (4), hypochondriasis (2), psychasthenia (1), and reactive depression (4). The mean number of days spent in the hospital was 52, the range

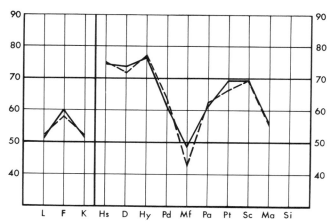

Figure 10. Neurosis (Female). *Solid Line:* Outpatients (N= 25, Mean Age 32, Age Range 17–56). *Broken Line:* Inpatients (N=24, Mean Age 24, Age Range 17–39).

being 20–114. Thirty-five per cent had a high school education or better, and 42 per cent were single.

Study 11: NEUROSIS (Schofield, 1956). *See Figure 11.*

The outpatient group were University of Wisconsin student outpatients. Their diagnoses were anxiety tension state (15), compulsive-obsessive (4), hysteria (2), and other (3). The inpatient group consisted of inpatient neurotics from the Psychopathic Unit of the University of Minnesota Hospitals. Diagnostic classification was psychoneurosis, mixed (3), psychoneurosis, reactive depression (5), and psychoneurosis, psychasthenia (2). The mean number of days spent in the hospital was 27; the range was 9–63. Seventy per cent had a high school education or better, and 30 per cent were single.

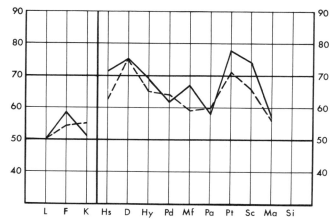

Figure 11. Neurosis (Male). *Solid Line:* Outpatients (N= 24, Mean Age 23, Age Range 19–29). *Broken Line:* Inpatients (N=10, Mean Age 36, Age Range 17–55).

Study 12: NEUROSIS (Silver and Sines, 1961). *See Figures 12a–12b.*

The subjects were drawn from the Fergus Falls (Minnesota) State Hospital population. All literate, testable, newly admitted patients under age 65 completed the MMPI within five days following admission to the hospital as part of a routine psychological test battery.

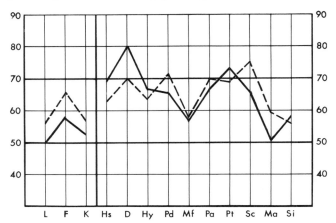

Figure 12a. Neurosis (Male). *Solid Line:* Neurotics (N=16). *Broken Line:* Comparison Schizophrenics (N=67).

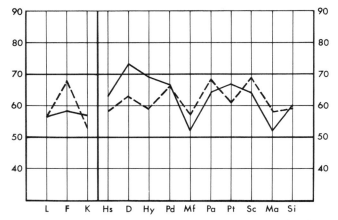

Figure 12b. Neurosis (Female). *Solid Line:* Neurotics (N=40). *Broken Line:* Comparison Schizophrenics (N=97).

About 10 per cent of the males and 20 per cent of the females were subsequently diagnosed neurotic. Diagnosis may have been influenced by the patient's MMPI characteristics. All patients tested who fell in this category were included, regardless of validity scale values. These subjects were compared with the acute schizophrenia sample described in Study 1.

Comparison showed that among the males the neurotic group scored lower than the schizophrenic group on the L, F, and Ma scales; and among the females the neurotic group scored higher than the schizophrenic group on the K, D, Hy, and Pt scales, and lower on the F, Mf (i.e., showed greater femininity), Pa, and Ma scales.

Study 13: NEUROSIS (Taulbee and Sisson, 1957). *See Figure 13.*

The subjects were VA psychiatric patients diagnosed psychoneurotic.

The outpatients were drawn from the Omaha Mental Hygiene Clinic. They were diagnosed independently of their MMPI results. The inpatients were drawn from the Omaha VA Hospital. The extent to which the MMPI

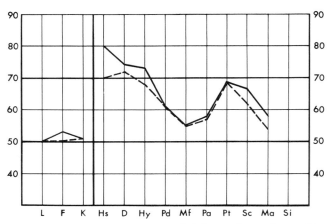

Figure 13. Neurosis (Male). *Solid Line:* Outpatients (N=90). *Broken Line:* Inpatients (N=40).

contributed to their diagnosis is not known, but it is believed that in the majority of cases diagnosis was minimally influenced by the MMPI findings.

The outpatients scored higher than the inpatients on the Hs and Hy scales.

Study 14: NEUROTIC REACTIONS (Hovey, 1949). *See Figures 14a–14b.*

The subjects were drawn from the 10 to 15 per cent of the general medical and surgical patients at the VA hospital in Salt Lake City who were referred for psychological evaluation over a seventeen-month period. The MMPI was administered to 446 of the patients so referred. For patients with less than a high school education the individual card form was usually employed. Cases were discarded if they showed up as probably

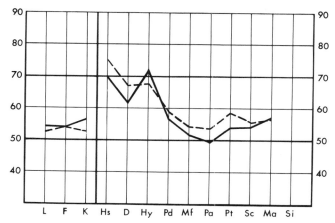

Figure 14a. Dissociative-Conversion and Somatization Reactions (Male). *Solid Line*: Dissociative-Conversion Reaction Group (N=34). *Broken Line*: Somatization Reaction Group (N=105).

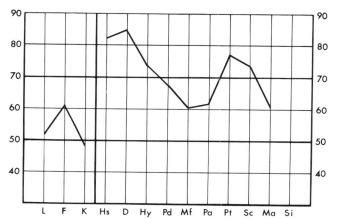

Figure 14b. Anxiety Reaction Group (Male, N=60).

"faking bad" according to Gough's F—K criterion, or if they achieved a T score of over 75 on the K scale.

The present groups consisted of those patients who were classified with a major psychiatric diagnosis of somatization reaction (including psychogenic gastrointestinal, cardiovascular, and the like), dissociative-conversion reaction, and anxiety reaction. Diagnosis was based on medical, psychiatric, social, and psychological studies, and observations of behavior while the subjects were hospitalized. Final psychiatric diagnosis was made by attending psychiatrists. The MMPI profiles may have had a bearing on the diagnoses in some cases, but only as supplementary data. They were not consulted in making final psychiatric diagnoses.

The dissociative-conversion group scored lower than the somatization group on the D, Pa, and Pt scales, and

lower than the anxiety group on the K, Hs, D, Pd, Mf, Pa, Pt, Sc, and Ma scales. The somatization group scored lower than the anxiety group on the K, Hs, D, Hy, Pd, Mf, Pa, Pt, Sc, and Ma scales.

Study 15: NEUROTIC REACTIONS (Rosen, 1958). *See Figures 15a–15b.*

The subjects were white veterans from the psychiatry service of the Minneapolis VA Hospital. All subjects had been tested within 15 days of admission and before any physical treatment. Only so-called "pure" cases were selected for the sample. Thus, a case was excluded if there was evidence that the patient had been given two different diagnoses upon successive admissions, or a diagnosis containing a statement of overlapping trends.

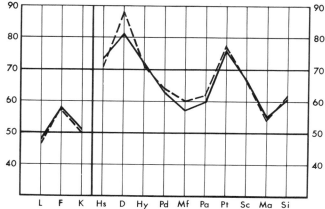

Figure 15a. Anxiety and Depressive Reactions (Male). *Solid Line*: Anxiety Reaction Group (N=83). *Broken Line*: Depressive Reaction Group (N=36).

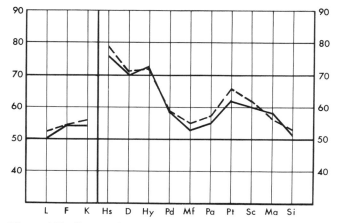

Figure 15b. Conversion and Somatization Reactions (Male). *Solid Line*: Conversion Reaction Group (N=49). *Broken Line*: Somatization Reaction Group (N=39).

21

The diagnostic categories were as follows: anxiety reaction (anxiety state); depressive reaction (neurotic depression); conversion reaction (conversion hysteria); and somatization reaction (psychophysiological reaction, psychosomatic reaction, organ neurosis).

The anxiety reaction group scored higher than the conversion reaction group on the D, Pd, Mf, Pa, Pt, Sc, and Si scales, and higher than the somatization reaction group on the D, Pt, and Si scales. The depressive reaction group scored higher than the anxiety reaction group on the D scale; higher than the conversion reaction group on the D, Pd, Mf, Pa, Pt, and Si scales; and higher than the somatization reaction group on the D, Mf, Pa, Pt, and Si scales. The conversion reaction group scored higher than the depressive reaction group on the Ma scale. The somatization reaction group scored higher than both the anxiety reaction group and the depressive reaction group on the L and K scales.

Personality Disorders

Study 16: ALCOHOLISM (Hoyt and Sedlacek, 1958). *See Figure 16.*

The alcoholic group was drawn from the Willmar (Minnesota) State Hospital (79 cases), and the Mental Health Institute, Independence, Iowa (98 cases). The subjects were white, with at least a fifth-grade education or its equivalent, and had received a diagnosis of chronic alcoholism by a physician and/or a clinical psychologist. The nonalcoholic group consisted of 50 male VA on-the-farm trainees who had no known personality disturbance.

Statistical comparisons were not made. However, the Pd scale was consistently the highest peaked scale for the alcoholic subjects.

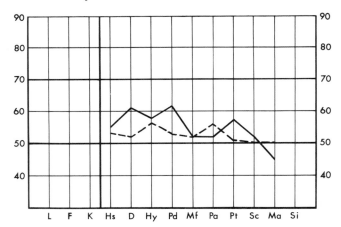

Figure 16. Alcoholism (Male). *Solid Line*: Alcoholics (N= 177). *Broken Line*: Nonalcoholics (N=50).

Study 17: ALCOHOLISM (Rosen, 1960). *See Figures 17a–17c.*

The Alcohol Clinic patients were consecutive admis-

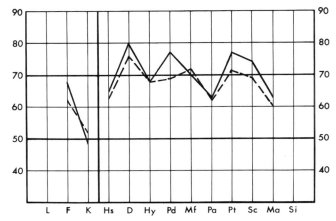

Figure 17a. Alcoholism (Male). *Solid Line*: Alcohol Clinic Patients (N=78, Mean Age 39, Mean IQ Bright Normal, Mean Education 11). *Broken Line*: Psychiatric Outpatients (N=35, Mean Age 32, Mean IQ Bright Normal, Mean Education 12).

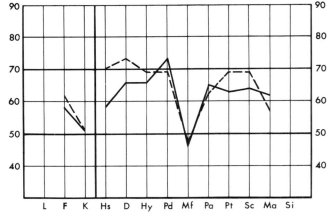

Figure 17b. Alcoholism (Female). *Solid Line*: Alcohol Clinic Patients (N=25). *Broken Line*: Psychiatric Outpatients (N=56).

sions to the Alcohol Clinic of the University of California at Los Angeles. Their average IQ was in the bright normal to superior range. The psychiatric outpatients were consecutive admissions to the UCLA Outpatient Psychiatric Clinic, and were drawn from the same geographical and socioeconomic areas as the Alcohol Clinic pa-

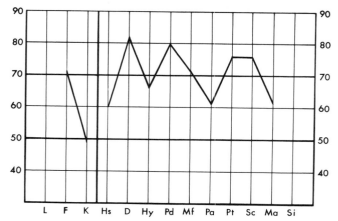

Figure 17c. Skid Row Alcoholics (Male, N=17).

tients. Their average IQ was in the bright normal range. The Skid Row alcoholics were alcoholics from the Los Angeles Skid Row section who had volunteered for a psychotherapeutic program. They were older than the preceding groups, had fewer years of schooling, and had made considerably lower vocational adjustment.

The male Alcohol Clinic patients scored higher than the male psychiatric outpatients on the F, Pd, and Pt scales. The male Alcohol Clinic patients did not differ from the Skid Row alcoholics on any of the scales. The female Alcohol Clinic patients scored higher than the female psychiatric outpatients on the Pd scale and lower on the Hs scale.

Study 18: TREATMENT OF ALCOHOLISM (Muzekari, 1965). *See Figure 18.*

The subjects were white males drawn from the files of the Fairview Alcoholic Rehabilitation Center, Ridgeway, South Carolina. Selection was made on the basis of completeness of test data and adequate follow-up information. Of the subjects, 108 were married, 31 were divorced, 16 were separated, and 25 were single. South Carolina residents constituted 93 per cent of the sample. The two groups did not differ significantly in age, IQ, education, or marital status.

The successful group consisted of those who main-

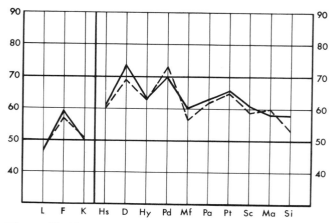

Figure 18. Treatment of Alcoholism (Male). *Solid Line:* Successful Group (N=86). *Broken Line:* Unsuccessful Group (N=94).

tained at least one year's sobriety after treatment, and the unsuccessful group consisted of those who did not meet this criterion.

The successful group scored higher than the unsuccessful group on the D, Mf, and Si scales (the originally reported validation and cross-validation groups are combined into a single sample in the present abstract). Several other statistical procedures showed minimal success in differentiating the two groups.

Study 19: ANTISOCIAL BEHAVIOR IN THE AGED (Apfeldorf, Scheinker, and Whitman, 1966). *See Figure 19.*

The subjects were members of a 400-bed domiciliary for aged male veterans. None had a known record of

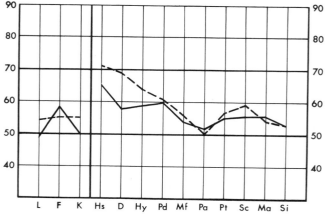

Figure 19. Antisocial Behavior in the Aged (Male). *Solid Line:* Offenders (N=22, Mean Age 63). *Broken Line:* Non-offenders (N=39, Mean Age 67).

psychiatric or neurological diagnosis, or a physical disability that would prevent their taking the MMPI. All subjects obtained a raw score of 19 or above on the vocabulary section of the Institute of Living Scale. The mean score on this scale was 30 for each group.

Offenders were those whose official records showed a clear-cut indication of antisocial behavior. This information was obtained either from domiciliary files or from police records in the neighboring town. Nonoffenders were those who had no such record of antisocial behavior, and who in addition were judged by the domiciliary director and social worker not to have engaged in antisocial activity.

The offenders scored lower than the nonoffenders on the L and K scales. There were no differences on the clinical scales.

Study 20: NARCOTIC ADDICTION (Hill, Haertzen, and Glaser, 1960). *See Figures 20a–20b.*

The subjects were former narcotic addicts who were undergoing rehabilitative therapy at the Public Health

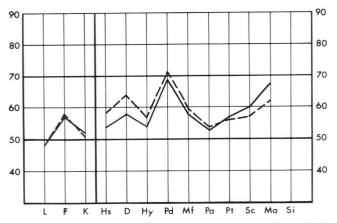

Figure 20a. Narcotic Addiction among Adults (Male). *Solid Line*: Negroes (N=70, Mean Age 26). *Broken Line*: Whites (N=88, Mean Age 37).

Service Hospital at Lexington, Kentucky, during 1951–52. They were tested approximately four to eight weeks following admission and recovery from withdrawal of opiates. None were deteriorated or overtly psychotic. Some were voluntary patients, the remainder prisoners who were serving sentences of one to ten years; these groups did not differ in their MMPI responses. Protocols with questionable scores on the validity scales were discarded.

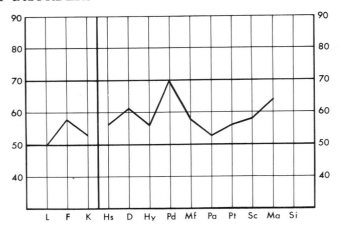

Figure 20b. Teenage Narcotic Addicts (Male, N=49).

Responses of adult Negroes and adult whites were recorded separately. The teenage group consisted of Negro and white addicts under 21, who were treated in a separate unit of the hospital.

Study 21: NARCOTIC ADDICTION (Olson, 1964). *See Figure 21.*

The subjects were adult addicts treated at the Patton (California) State Hospital (males), and the California Institution for Women at Frontera (females). None were

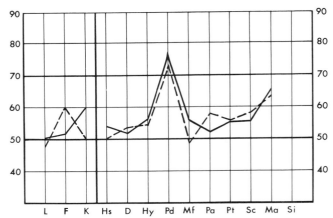

Figure 21. Narcotic Addiction. *Solid Line*: Male Addicts (N=60, Mean Age 29, Mean IQ approx. 90). *Broken Line*: Female Addicts (N=60, Mean Age 28, Mean IQ approx. 96).

overtly psychotic or deteriorated, and none were suffering from withdrawal symptoms at the time of testing. Nearly all had a diagnosis of sociopathic personality disturbance, and all were addicted to heroin except for seven males who were addicted to other medically obtainable drugs. Slightly less than one half of the subjects were of Mexican-American extraction.

The males scored higher than the females on the K scale and lower on the Pa scale.

Study 22: PERSONALITY DISORDER (Silver and Sines, 1961). *See Figures 22a–22b.*

The subjects were drawn from the Fergus Falls (Minnesota) State Hospital population. All literate, testable, newly admitted patients under age 65 completed the MMPI within five days following admission to the hos-

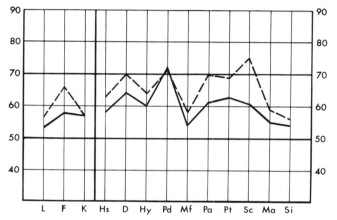

Figure 22a. Personality Disorder (Male). *Solid Line*: Personality Disorder Group (N=54). *Broken Line*: Acute Schizophrenia Comparison Group (N=67).

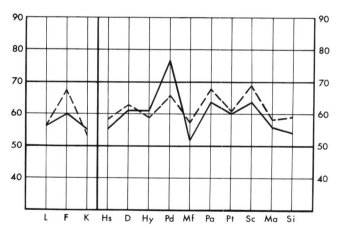

Figure 22b. Personality Disorder (Female). *Solid Line*: Personality Disorder Group (N=22). *Broken Line*: Acute Schizophrenia Comparison Group (N=97).

pital as part of a routine psychological test battery. Those subsequently diagnosed personality disorder were included in the present sample (about 30 per cent of those tested for males, and about 10 per cent for females). Diagnosis may have been influenced by the patient's MMPI characteristics.

Subjects were compared with the acute schizophrenia groups described in Study 1.

The male personality disorder group scored higher than the male schizophrenia group on the Es scale and lower on the L, F, Hs, Hy, Mf, Pa, Pt, and Sc scales. The female personality disorder group scored higher than the female schizophrenia group on the Pd scale and lower on the F, Mf, and Si scales.

Study 23: PSYCHOPATHIC PERSONALITY (Guthrie, 1950). *See Figure 23.*

The subjects were patients in a mental hospital and in a veterans' hospital in Ontario, Canada. They had been hospitalized for a variety of reasons which included alcoholism, court referral, and anxiety complaints. Almost all had a history of minor delinquency, unsteady work, and poor home relations. Summaries emphasized that few had profited from treatment. Only those patients on whom there was complete agreement among the diagnostic staff regarding diagnosis were included. The influence of the psychometric findings on the diagnosis was minimal since the diagnosis of the psychiatrist was recorded before the psychometric findings were presented.

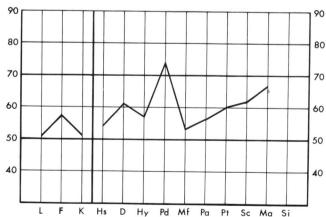

Figure 23. Psychopathic Personality Group (Male, N=25).

Study 24: EFFECT OF PROMAZINE (Sulzer, 1961). *See Figure 24.*

The subjects were psychiatric patients who were known to have been schizophrenic for at least one year, and who had shown no significant clinical indications of improvement during hospitalization. All were 45 years of age or younger, and none had any major secondary diagnosis or significant physical disease. All drug administration was controlled in a double blind design.

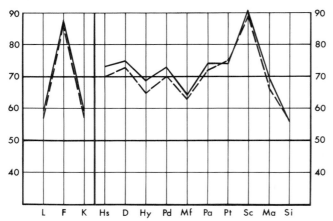

Figure 24. Effect of Promazine (Male, N=41). *Solid Line:* Post-Promazine Tests. *Broken Line:* Post-Placebo Tests.

The study was divided into several periods of five to seven weeks, during which patients were alternately given promazine and a placebo. Patients were tested with the MMPI after each period of promazine or placebo, so that most patients completed it four times, two after promazine and two after placebo. All post-promazine tests were combined, and all post-placebo tests were combined.

The promazine tests did not differ from the placebo tests on any scale.

Study 25: PREDICTION OF HOSPITALIZATION (Peterson, 1954b). *See Figure 25.*

The subjects were veterans who had attended the VA Mental Hygiene Clinic, St. Paul, Minnesota, at some time during the period from 1947 through 1951. They had all been given psychological tests and had been interviewed two or more times. All had a service-connected psychiatric disability, "service-connected" being defined broadly to include origin of a neuropsychiatric disorder, aggravation of such a disorder, or emotional contribution to some nonpsychiatric disability. Nearly all the patients were white and lived in the vicinity of Minneapolis and

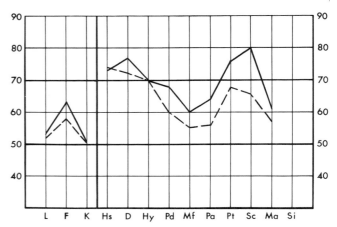

Figure 25. Prediction of Hospitalization (Male). *Solid Line:* Hospitalized Group (N=108). *Broken Line:* Nonhospitalized Group (N=114).

St. Paul. There were veterans from both world wars but they were primarily from the second. Almost all had had psychotherapy, mainly with psychiatric residents and less often with clinical psychology trainees and social workers.

The hospitalized group consisted of those patients who had been admitted to the hospital after examination, while the nonhospitalized group had not been admitted.

Study 26: FACTORS IN PSYCHOTHERAPY (Sullivan, Miller, and Smelser, 1958). *See Figures 26a–26b.*

The subjects were white veterans of World War II or the Korean War who were patients at the VA Mental Hygiene Clinic, Oakland, California. All had completed the MMPI at the time of initial contact with the clinic. About 25 per cent of the patients were schizophrenic, the remainder being psychoneurotic and psychosomatic cases. The data were gathered between 1951 and 1955. A number of demographic and therapist measures were also investigated: patient's age, education, occupation, and therapist's sex, professional discipline, and experience. There were 83 subjects altogether.

With regard to length of stay in therapy, subjects were divided at the median in terms of the number of individ-

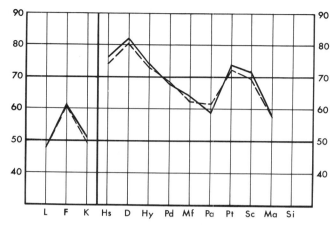

Figure 26a. Length of Stay in Psychotherapy (Male). *Solid Line*: Stay Group (N=approx. 40, Mean Age 33). *Broken Line*: Nonstay Group (N=approx. 40, Mean Age 31).

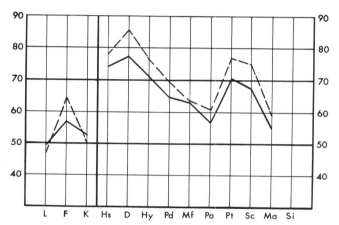

Figure 26b. Improvement after Therapy (Male). *Solid Line*: Improved Group (N=approx. 40, Mean Age 31). *Broken Line*: Unimproved Group (N=approx. 40, Mean Age 31).

ual therapy sessions they received, and the two groups were designated stay and nonstay. To determine improvement, ratings on a five-point scale were made by individual therapists after termination of therapy. Those patients receiving the three lowest points on the rating scale were designated as unimproved, the others as improved.

There were no MMPI differences between the groups classified by length of stay. The improved subjects scored lower than the unimproved group on the F, Hs, D, Hy, Pd, Pt, Sc, Ma, and A scales. Demographic variables discriminated between stayers and nonstayers, with the stayers being younger, better educated, and of higher occupational level. Occupational level also discriminated between the improved and unimproved groups.

Study 27: PROGNOSIS IN PSYCHOTHERAPY (Barron, 1953b). *See Figure 27.*

The subjects were adult neurotics who subsequently underwent six months of psychotherapy in the outpatient service of a state psychiatric clinic. The MMPI was administered before therapy. The patients were receiving psychotherapy for the first time and they began the treatment just as their therapists were starting a six-month period of service in the outpatient clinic. The therapists were psychiatric residents with little experience in intensive psychotherapy. The patients, 12 men and 21 women, were given one hour of treatment a week for six months. All but 3 were high school graduates, but only 2 were college graduates. As a group they could probably be characterized as lower middle class. Two-thirds were gainfully employed. Their age range was 20–45.

All subjects were rated after treatment as improved or unimproved by two expert judges who had had no part in the conduct of the therapy. Each therapist made a formal presentation before the two judges of every case he had handled; before the presentation, the judges had read all the material concerning the patients which had been recorded in the clinical chart.

The unimproved group scored higher than the improved group on the Pa scale.

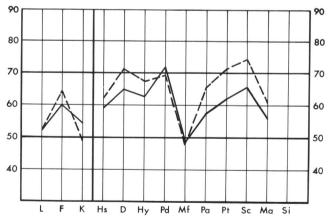

Figure 27. Prognosis in Psychotherapy (Male and Female). *Solid Line*: Improved Group (N=17). *Broken Line*: Unimproved Group (N=16). Note: The Mf scores shown were for females; for males they were 62 (improved) and 67 (unimproved).

Study 28: SHOCK THERAPY (Feldman, 1952). *See Figures 28a–28b.*

The subjects were patients at the Langley Porter Neuropsychiatric Institute in San Francisco, who were given

27

the MMPI before shock treatment between the years 1943 and 1948 and who were diagnosed either schizophrenia or affective disorder. Records were eliminated if they did not contain at least one T score of 70 or above, other than Mf, or if they were judged invalid (T score

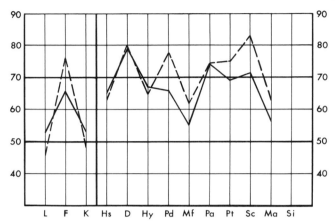

Figure 28a. Effect of Shock Therapy on Schizophrenia (Male and Female). *Solid Line*: Recovered Group (N=34). *Broken Line*: Unimproved Group (N=24).

above 70 on the cannot say scale or a raw score above 19 on the F scale). Three types of shock treatment — electric shock, electronarcosis, and insulin — were used, with the majority of the patients receiving electric shock.

The patients were grouped according to psychiatrists' ratings of improvement at the termination of treatment and at a follow-up at least six months later. Records were eliminated if the two ratings were inconsistent. The patients with consistent ratings were divided into three

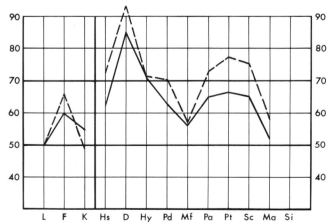

Figure 28b. Effect of Shock Therapy on Affective Disorder (Male and Female). *Solid Line*: Recovered Group (N=52). *Broken Line*: Unimproved Group (N=10).

groups: recovered, improved, and unimproved. The recovered and unimproved groups are presented here.

Study 29: SEVERITY OF PSYCHOPATHOLOGY (Shaffer, Ota, and Hanlon, 1964). *See Figures 29a–29b.*

The subjects were all recently hospitalized, acutely disturbed psychiatric patients referred for pre-treatment evaluation in connection with an ongoing investigation of the comparative effectiveness of various tranquilizing drugs. Patients were referred on the basis of target symp-

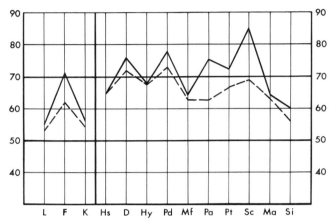

Figure 29a. Severity of Psychopathology (Male). *Solid Line*: High Morbidity Group (N=31). *Broken Line*: Low Morbidity Group (N=31).

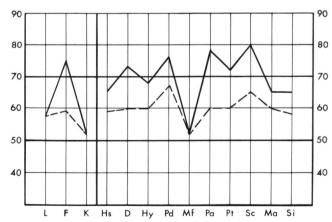

Figure 29b. Severity of Psychopathology (Female). *Solid Line*: High Morbidity Group (N=35). *Broken Line*: Low Morbidity Group (N=35).

toms such as anxiety, agitation, and restlessness without reference to the usual nosologic considerations; the majority, however, carried schizophrenic diagnoses. Alcoholics, seniles, those under court order, and those with chronic brain syndromes or major organic diseases were excluded. The total sample consisted of 90 males and 104 females ranging in age from 18 to 61 years. Each patient was rated for severity of psychopathology using the Multi-dimensional Scale for Rating Psychiatric Patients, from which a Total Morbidity score was derived. All patients were rated by one of four clinical psychologists, each having had wide experience with disturbed patients as well as with the instrument. The ward observation section of the instrument was completed by nursing personnel specially trained to perform this task. All patients were rated shortly after a 48-hour drug-free interval and before administration of any phrenotropic medication. The individual form of the MMPI was given on the same day the ratings were made, usually within a few hours of the latter. The MMPI was not administered by the psychologists making the ratings and all ratings were made without knowledge of the test results.

The high morbidity and low morbidity groups consisted of the top and bottom thirds of the distribution on the Total Morbidity score. The mean age of the males was 35, and the mean age of the females was 37.

The male high morbidity group scored higher than the male low morbidity group on the F, Pa, and Sc scales. The female high morbidity group scored higher than the female low morbidity group on the F, Hs, D, Hy, Pd, Pa, Pt, Sc, Si, and A scales.

Study 30: SUICIDE (Farberow, 1950). *See Figure 30.*

The subjects were patients in a VA mental hospital, and had been placed on a continual observation ward be-

cause of suspected suicidal tendencies. They were tested on their entrance to the ward. There were additional patients who were not included because they were not amenable to testing. Both of the groups shown here had spent approximately the same length of time in the hospital before being tested, and they were approximately the same in age, religious distribution, and occupational status. About half of each group had a high school education.

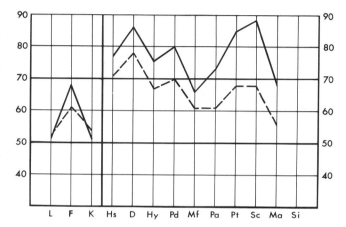

Figure 30. Suicide (Male). *Solid Line*: Threat Group (N=32). *Broken Line*: Attempt Group (N=32).

The attempt group consisted of those who had actually made an abortive attempt at suicide. The threat group consisted of those who had threatened suicide but had not yet attempted it.

The threat group scored higher than the attempt group on the F, D, Pd, Pa, Pt, Sc, and Ma scales.

Psychophysiological and Physical Disorders

Study 31: GASTRIC ULCER (Sullivan and Welsh, 1952). *See Figure 31.*

The subjects were patients at a VA mental hygiene clinic.

The ulcer group consisted of patients who were known to have gastric ulcers. The control group consisted of randomly selected patients.

Configural analysis performed between half of the ulcer group and a second control group (not reproduced

here), and validated by comparing the remaining ulcer patients with the original control group, yielded the following relationships which discriminated the ulcer patients from the control group: The ulcer patients had higher scores on the Hs scale than on the D, Hy, Pt, and Sc scales, and higher scores on the D scale than on the Hy scale. A cutting point between two and three of the six signs discriminated the validation groups beyond the .001 level.

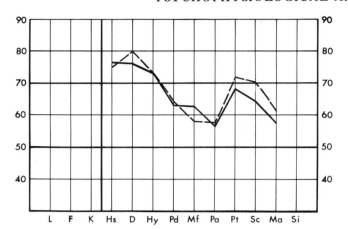

Figure 31. Gastric Ulcer (Male). *Solid Line*: Ulcer Group (N=60). *Broken Line*: Control Group (N=30).

Study 32: LOW BACK PAIN (Hanvik, 1951). *See Figure 32.*

The subjects were patients admitted to the Minneapolis VA Hospital, with back pain the primary reason for hospitalization. The pain originated or appeared to originate in the back, in the spinal column, or in close proximity thereto, from the lowest thoracic vertebrae to the coccyx. There frequently was other pain (radiated or associated), but the source of pain was deemed to be the lower back. The subjects ranged in age from 20 to 55, with a median age of 35.

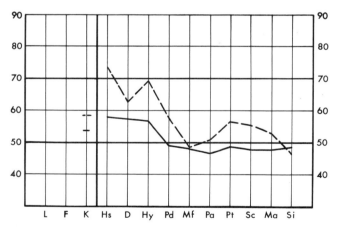

Figure 32. Low Back Pain (Male). *Solid Line*: Organic Group (N=30). *Broken Line*: Functional Group (N=30).

The organic group consisted of patients with protruded intervertebral disc, and in all but two the evidence was surgical, i.e., a disc was removed in an operation. In the other two cases the diagnosis was based on X-ray evi-

dence (spinogram) and characteristic history, plus evidence of correctly distributed pain. About half were tested before surgery, and half afterward. There were no significant MMPI differences between those tested before and those tested afterward. The functional group consisted of patients for whom there were no clear-cut medical findings; i.e., the general physical and neurological examinations were essentially negative.

The functional group scored higher than the organic group on the Hs, D, Hy, Pd, Pt, and Sc scales.

Study 33: MEDICAL DISABILITIES (Wiener, 1952). *See Figures 33a–33b.*

The subjects were drawn from the records of disabled veterans who had completed counseling in the Minnesota VA program during 1946 through 1948.

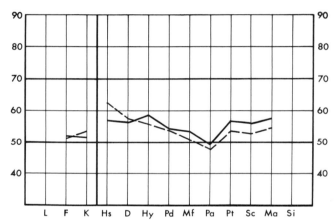

Figure 33a. Medical Disabilities (Male). *Solid Line*: Skin Disorder Group (N=50, Mean Age 26, Mean Education 11.0). *Broken Line*: Ulcer Group (N=50, Mean Age 30, Mean Education 10.6).

The skin disorder group consisted of veterans with varying degrees and locations of skin outbreaks, ranging from disorders covering the whole body to those limited to hands or feet. The ulcer group consisted of veterans with the diagnoses of peptic, gastric, duodenal, and stomach ulcer or ulcers. They were significantly older than the no disability group, and were significantly lower in education and intelligence. The asthma group consisted of veterans with diagnosed bronchial asthma. They were significantly lower than the no disability group in intelligence and education. The no disability group consisted of nondisabled veterans who completed counseling under

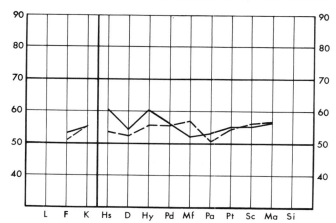

Figure 33b. Medical Disabilities (Male). *Solid Line*: Asthma Group (N=50, Mean Age 26, Mean Education 10.5). *Broken Line*: No Disability Group (N=100, Mean Age 24, Mean Education 11.7).

the GI Bill in 1946 and 1947 at VA guidance centers. The selection of cases was more or less random.

Study 34: OBESITY (Levitt and Fellner, 1965). *See Figure 34.*

The subjects had come to the hospital of their own accord for weight reduction, and were drawn from the first 28 obese women who were able and willing to participate in the study. While going through the prescribed treatment they were routinely administered the MMPI. Upon discharge they were assigned to one of three groups.

The simple group consisted of women who lost weight quite satisfactorily when in a hospital setting they were placed on a simple diet to restrict calories. The metabolic group consisted of women who had a strong family his-

tory of obesity; and each subject had been obese for a long period of years. Such people lose weight with great difficulty by simple dietary restriction and many will not lose at all for periods of many weeks. (The third, mixed, group is omitted from the present abstract.) None of the subjects knew of their obesity classification at the time they took the MMPI.

The simple group scored higher than the metabolic group on the Hy, Pt, Sc, and Ma scales, and lower on the Mf scale (i.e., showed greater femininity).

Study 35: PHYSICAL INJURY (Motto, 1958). *See Figure 35.*

The subjects were drawn at random from male counseling cases seen over a three-year period at a Detroit VA counseling service for disabled veterans. Cases of psychosomatic disorders such as asthma, neurodermatitis, ulcers, and colitis were not included, nor were cases where there was unmistakable evidence of neurological involvement, nor were cases with both physical and psychogenic difficulties.

The physical injury group consisted of veterans having VA ratings for tuberculosis (32), or for gunshot wounds or amputations (18). The schizophrenia control group consisted of veterans having VA ratings for schizophrenia. The composition by types was as follows: unclassified (20), paranoid (13), catatonic (11), simple (3), and mixed (3).

The schizophrenic group scored higher than the physical injury group on the Pa, Pt, and Sc scales.

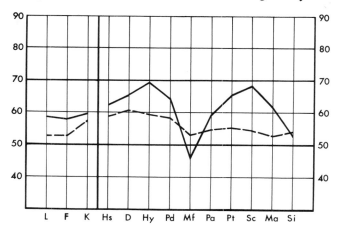

Figure 34. Obesity (Female). *Solid Line*: Simple Group (N=7). *Broken Line*: Metabolic Group (N=9).

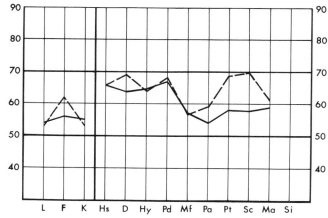

Figure 35. Physical Injury (Male). *Solid Line*: Physical Injury Group (N=50, Mean Age 28, Mean Education 10.1). *Broken Line*: Schizophrenia Group (N=50, Mean Age 29, Mean Education 10.1).

Study 36: APHASIA (Doehring and Reitan, 1960). *See Figure 36.*

The aphasic subjects consisted of brain-damaged white patients with aphasic symptoms. There were three patients with intrinsic cerebral tumors, seven with traumatic head injuries, two with cerebral vascular disease, one with multiple sclerosis, one with cerebral abscess, one with subdural hematoma, one with chronic brain syndrome, and one with excision of the left temporal lobe

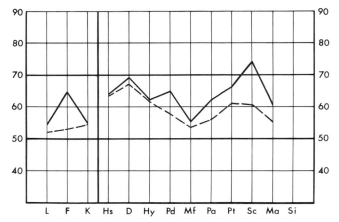

Figure 36. Aphasia (Male). *Solid Line*: Aphasics (N=17, Mean Age 34, Mean Education 10). *Broken Line*: Nonaphasics (N=17, Mean Age 35, Mean Education 11).

for relief of epilepsy. The nonaphasic control group consisted of brain-damaged patients with no aphasic symptoms. There were three patients with intrinsic cerebral tumors, eight with traumatic head injuries, two with cerebral vascular disease, two with multiple sclerosis, one with chronic brain syndrome, and one with excision of the left temporal lobe for relief of epilepsy. Presence or absence of aphasic symptoms was determined by evaluation of the Halstead-Wepman Screening Test. The groups were matched with respect to age, years of education, and type of brain lesion.

The aphasic group scored higher than the nonaphasic group on the F, Pd, and Sc scales.

Study 37: BRAIN LESIONS (Andersen and Hanvik, 1950). *See Figure 37.*

The subjects were patients at the Minneapolis VA Hospital. All had suffered focal brain damage, and the

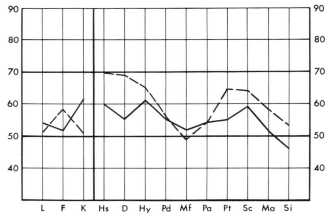

Figure 37. Brain Lesions (Male). *Solid Line*: Frontal Group (N=16). *Broken Line*: Parietal Group (N=27).

locus of the lesion had been ascertained either by surgery (e.g., in cases of brain tumor) or in gunshot wound cases by X-ray demonstration of metallic foreign bodies in the brain.

In the frontal group, the lesions were confined to the frontal lobes. In the parietal group, some patients had lesions which extended to more than one lobe, although in all cases there was the common denominator of "parietal involvement." With respect to laterality, there were approximately the same number of right and left hemisphere lesions.

The frontal group scored higher than the parietal group on the K scale, and lower on the D, Pt, and Si scales.

Study 38: EPILEPSY (Klove and Doehring, 1962). *See Figures 38a–38b.*

The subjects had epileptic disorders or adjustment difficulties of a comparable nature. None of the subjects were taken from chronic institutionalized populations. The individual form of the MMPI was used.

The lesion with epilepsy group consisted of 18 males and 2 females in whom epilepsy was associated with known neurologic disorders. It included 2 patients with cerebral abscess, 2 with arteriovenous malformation, 2 with cerebro-vascular accident, 9 with closed head injury, and 5 with chronic brain lesion. Of these patients, 10 had grand mal seizures, 5 had psychomotor seizures, 4 had both grand mal and psychomotor seizures, and 1 had

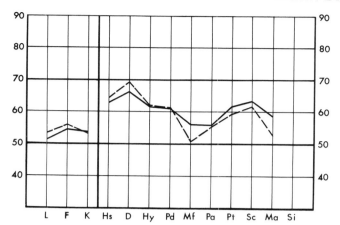

Figure 38a. Epilepsy and Lesions (Male and Female). *Solid Line*: Lesion with Epilepsy Group (N=20, Mean Age 35, Mean Education 10.0). *Broken Line*: Lesion without Epilepsy Group (N=20, Mean Age 34, Mean Education 10.2).

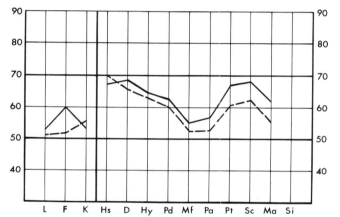

Figure 38b. Epilepsy and Medical Disorders (Male and Female). *Solid Line*: Epilepsy without Lesion Group (N=20, Mean Age 34, Mean Education 10.8). *Broken Line*: Medical Patients (N=20, Mean Age 34, Mean Education 10.6).

both grand mal and Jacksonian seizures. The lesion without epilepsy group consisted of 19 males and 1 female with brain damage unaccompanied by epilepsy. It included 1 patient with cerebral abscess, 2 with cerebrovascular accident, 2 with arteriovenous malformation, 2 with penetrating head injury, 2 with closed head injury, 4 with chronic brain lesion, and 6 with multiple sclerosis. The cause of the lesion in the remaining patient was not reported. The epilepsy without lesion group consisted of 16 males and 4 females with epilepsy unaccompanied by a history of neurologic disorder to which the epileptic condition might be attributed. It included 5 patients with grand mal seizures, 7 with psychomotor seizures, 6 with both grand mal and psychomotor seizures, and 2 with

both grand mal and Jacksonian seizures. The medical patient control group consisted of 19 males and 1 female with primary organic complaints other than cerebral disease. It included 13 paraplegics, 2 diabetics, and 1 patient each with breast carcinoma, spinal disc surgery, occipital osteoma, optic neuritis, and axillary nerve surgery. Such a group might be expected to have adjustment difficulties somewhat comparable to the adjustment difficulties experienced by epileptics.

There were no over-all differences among the groups (as tested by analysis of variance, which also included a fifth group) or with respect to the proportion of subjects scoring highest on a given scale.

Study 39: MULTIPLE SCLEROSIS (Canter, 1951). *See Figure 39.*

The subjects were fairly representative of World War II veterans in the early stages of multiple sclerosis. The duration of the acute symptoms ranged from one to eight years, with an approximate average of four years. In all cases sufficient organic damage existed to make the medical diagnosis of multiple sclerosis certain. The group form of the MMPI was administered as part of a battery of psychological tests.

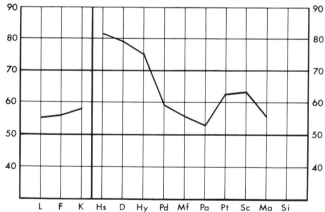

Figure 39. Group with Multiple Sclerosis at Early Stages (Male, N=83, Mean Age approx. 32).

Study 40: MULTIPLE SCLEROSIS (Gilberstadt and Farkas, 1961). *See Figure 40.*

The subjects were male veterans hospitalized on the Neurology Service of the Minneapolis VA Hospital. They had received a medical diagnosis of either multiple sclerosis or traumatic brain injury. Except for three cases of multiple sclerosis, the samples included all the patients

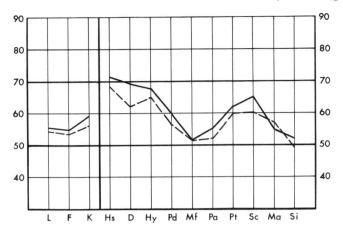

Figure 40. Multiple Sclerosis (Male). *Solid Line*: Multiple Sclerosis Group (N=25, Mean Age 33, Mean IQ 102). *Broken Line*: Traumatic Brain Injury Group (N=25, Mean Age 31, Mean IQ 103).

with these diagnoses who had been administered the MMPI and the Wechsler-Bellevue Intelligence Scale on the Neurology Service during the years 1949–52. The mean duration of illness of the multiple sclerosis sample was 58 months compared with 30 months for the brain injury group; this difference is significant.

The multiple sclerosis group scored higher than the brain injury group on the D and Sc scales.

Study 41: MULTIPLE SCLEROSIS (Shontz, 1955). *See Figure 41.*

The subjects were hospital patients. A shortened form

of the MMPI (including only those items relevant to the usual scales) was prepared, and this form was administered orally.

The multiple sclerosis group consisted of seven male and nine female patients who had been hospitalized specifically for multiple sclerosis. The chronic illness control group consisted of eight male and eight female patients

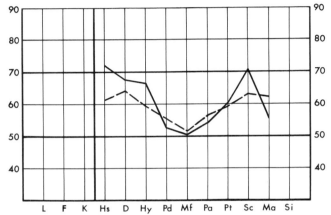

Figure 41. Multiple Sclerosis (Male and Female). *Solid Line*: Multiple Sclerosis Group (N=16, Mean Age 41). *Broken Line*: Chronic Illness Group (N=16, Mean Age 40).

matched for age but otherwise selected at random from a population of persons hospitalized for chronic illnesses other than multiple sclerosis.

The multiple sclerosis group scored higher than the chronic illness group on the Hs and Hy scales.

Adolescents, Delinquent and Disturbed

Study 42: DELINQUENCY IN AN AREA OF SMALL POPULATION (Ashbaugh, 1953). *See Figures 42a–42b.*

The delinquent boys and girls were selected from referrals to the juvenile court of Benton County, Oregon. A delinquent was defined as "any child whose conduct deviated sufficiently from normal social usage to warrant his being considered a menace to himself, his future life, or to society itself." The nondelinquent or control samples were drawn from the high schools of four coun-

ties. Honor pupils and class leaders were omitted because delinquency is uncommon among them. The nondelinquents were matched with the delinquents for sex, age, and residence in urban or rural areas. Twenty per cent were from rural areas and 80 per cent from urban areas. Subjects were eliminated if they achieved T scores of 70 or above on the L or F scales. The median age of the combined groups was 15.

Among the boys the delinquents scored higher than the nondelinquents on the Pd, Pa, Pt, Sc, and Ma scales.

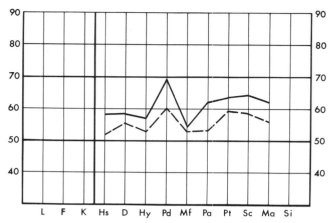

Figure 42a. Delinquency (Male). *Solid Line*: Delinquents (N=37). *Broken Line*: Nondelinquents (N=37).

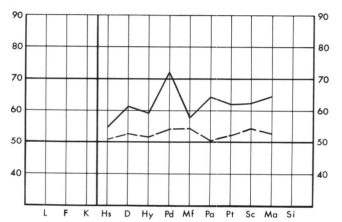

Figure 42b. Delinquency (Female). *Solid Line*: Delinquents (N=13). *Broken Line*: Nondelinquents (N=13).

Among the girls the delinquents scored higher than the nondelinquents on the Pd, Pa, Pt, and Ma scales.

Study 43: DELINQUENCY (Ball, 1962). *See Figures 43a–43b.*

The delinquent groups came from the Kentucky State Training School, and consisted of those of the 302 boys and 102 girls who were deemed capable of understanding and completing the MMPI items. Their mean IQ was about 99, as compared with 75–80 for the training school population as a whole. There were no Negroes in the sample. The nondelinquent groups consisted of virtually the entire ninth grade of two public school systems in Kentucky. About 15 per cent of the sample were Negroes (see Study 82). The two towns from which the sample was selected had populations between 10,000 and 19,-

000, and were comparable in most respects to other urban areas of similar size in Kentucky. It was pointed out that striking contrasts exist between urban and rural areas throughout Kentucky. The delinquent groups were

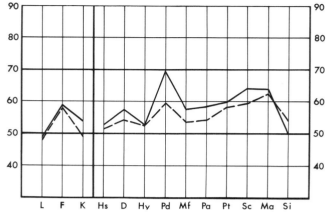

Figure 43a. Delinquency (Male). *Solid Line*: Delinquents (N=19, Mean Age 16.0, Age Range 13–18, Mean IQ 99). *Broken Line*: Nondelinquents (N=95, Mean Age 15.0, Age Range 13–18, Mean IQ 104).

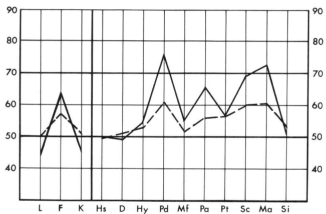

Figure 43b. Delinquency (Female). *Solid Line*: Delinquents (N=15, Mean Age 15.8, Age Range 13–18, Mean IQ approx. 99). *Broken Line*: Nondelinquents (N=105, Mean Age 14.8, Age Range 13–18, Mean IQ approx. 104).

characterized by significantly more educational retardation than the nondelinquent groups, and tended more often to come from lower socioeconomic classes and broken homes.

Among the boys the delinquents scored higher than the nondelinquents on the K and Pd scales. Among the girls the delinquents scored higher than the nondelinquents on the L, F, K, Pd, Pa, Sc, and Ma scales.

35

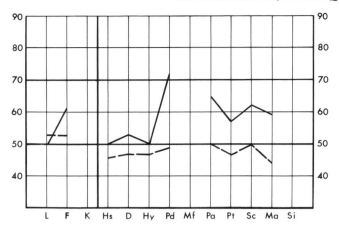

Figure 44. Delinquency (Female). *Solid Line*: Delinquents (N=99, Mean IQ 87). *Broken Line*: Nondelinquents (N=85, Mean IQ 101). Note: This profile is not K-corrected.

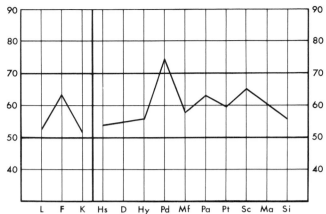

Figure 45. Delinquents (Female, N=170, Mean Age approx. 16, Age Range 13–18, Mean IQ approx. 88).

Study 44: DELINQUENCY (Capwell, 1945). *See Figure 44.*

The delinquent girls were drawn from the Minnesota State School for girls. The nondelinquent girls were drawn from the public schools of Sauk Centre, Minnesota. Both groups showed some retardation in school achievement when compared with the norms of the Stanford Achievement Test.

Every scale but Hy showed a significant difference between the groups. In order to control for differences in intelligence, delinquents were matched within two IQ points with 52 of the nondelinquents. The mean IQ of both matched groups was 95. The MMPI continued to differentiate the delinquents and nondelinquents reliably except for the Hs scale. The Hy scale was not examined since it did not differentiate the larger groups.

Study 45: DELINQUENCY (Jurjevich, 1963). *See Figure 45.*

The subjects were institutionalized delinquent girls. The MMPI was administered at least one month after admission, in order to allow a period of recovery from the trauma of court procedure and commitment. Records were rejected if the F scale raw score was 18 or more, and if F minus K was 7 or more. Subjects were instructed to answer all questions, and those who gave inadequate cooperation were asked to take the test a second time. For many subjects the test was administered in two sessions, in order to avoid fatigue. All subjects included in the study had an IQ score above 75.

Study 46: DELINQUENT AND DISTURBED BOYS (Rowley and Stone, 1962). *See Figure 46.*

The delinquent group were residents at the Iowa Training School for Boys at Eldora. The emotionally disturbed group were referred to the Child Psychiatry Services at the State University of Iowa. They represented a wide range of common child psychiatric problems as manifested by "neurotic" symptoms, stealing, lying, truancy, rebelliousness, school phobias, withdrawal, poor school-work, somatic complaints, and sexual difficulties. The socioeconomic status of the fathers of this group was higher than that of the delinquent group. Neither group contained boys who were judged mentally defective or who were suspected of brain injury. No subject over the

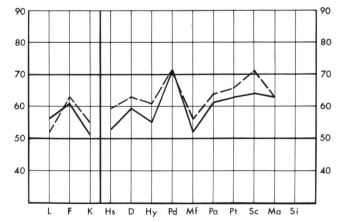

Figure 46. Delinquency and Emotional Disturbance (Male). *Solid Line*: Delinquents (N=60, Mean Age 15.1, Mean IQ 97, Mean Education 8.4). *Broken Line*: Emotionally Disturbed Group (N=60, Mean Age 14.8, Mean IQ approx. 103, Mean Education 8.5).

age of 16 was included in either group because of the 16-year age limit for the Child Psychiatry Services. One subject from each group was eliminated because of an invalid F scale (T score above 80). All subjects were tested in an institutional setting with the booklet form of the MMPI.

The delinquent group scored higher than the emotionally disturbed group on the L scale and lower on the K, Hs, Hy, Mf and Sc scales.

Study 47: DELINQUENT AND DISTURBED GIRLS (Stone and Rowley, 1963). *See Figure 47.*

The delinquent group consisted of girls from the Iowa State Training School for Girls at Mitchellville. The majority of these girls had been committed because of sexual misbehavior, vagrancy, or incorrigibility. At the time of testing the period of incarceration varied from several weeks to several months. Four girls were excluded from the sample because of an invalid F score (T score above 80). The emotionally disturbed group was drawn from girls who had given valid MMPI profiles at the Iowa State Psychopathic Hospital either on their first outpatient visit or immediately after hospitalization. These girls were selected by age to match the delinquents. They had been referred to the hospital because of various symptoms of emotional disturbance — behavior problems at home or at school, poor schoolwork, school phobia, withdrawal, depression, somatic complaints, and sexual difficulties. Neither group contained girls who

were mentally defective or suspected of brain damage. Socioeconomic factors were not controlled, and it was suspected that the emotionally disturbed group might have been from a higher socioeconomic level.

The delinquent girls scored higher than the emotionally disturbed girls on the Pd, Pa, Pt, and Ma scales and lower on the L, K, Hs, D, and Hy scales.

Study 48: SOCIAL AND SOLITARY DELINQUENTS (Randolph, Richardson, and Johnson, 1961). *See Figure 48.*

The subjects were boys who had been adjudged legally as juvenile delinquents. Most were at a "ranch" for delinquent boys, and the remainder were in custody, awaiting placement at this ranch. All were of at least dull normal intelligence.

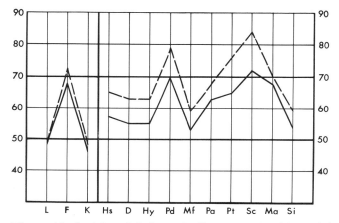

Figure 48. Social and Solitary Delinquency (Male). *Solid Line:* Social Delinquents (N=39, Age Range 14–18, Mean IQ 93). *Broken Line:* Solitary Delinquents (N=18, Age Range 14–18, Mean IQ 105).

The boys were judged from their delinquency histories as always having been either social or solitary in their known delinquencies. Four boys were excluded from the study because their delinquency histories were mixed (social and solitary). The solitary delinquents had a significantly higher mean IQ than the social delinquents and tended to come from higher socioeconomic levels.

The solitary delinquents scored higher than the social delinquents on Hs, D, Hy, Pd, Mf, Pa, Pt, Sc, and Si.

Study 49: TREATMENT OF DELINQUENT GIRLS (Lauber and Dahlstrom, 1953). *See Figure 49.*

The subjects were selected from among the 45 girls cared for during 1949–50 at Namequa Lodge, a resident

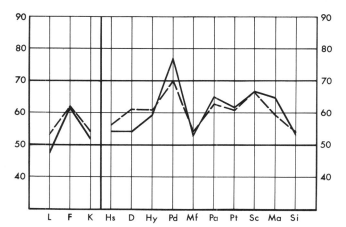

Figure 47. Delinquency and Emotional Disturbance (Female). *Solid Line:* Delinquents (N=60, Mean Age 15.6, Age Range 13–17, Mean IQ 100). *Broken Line:* Emotionally Disturbed Group (N=60, Mean Age 15.5, Age Range 13–17, Mean IQ approx. 95–100).

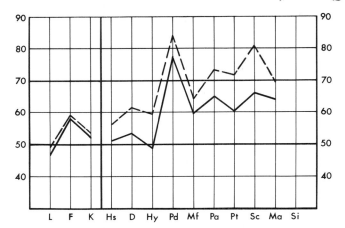

Figure 49. Treatment of Delinquent Girls. *Solid Line*: Success Group (N=17). *Broken Line*: Failure Group (N=18).

center for the care and education of problem girls in Illinois. All admissions were made through the Rock Island Juvenile Court. The institution used a plan of self-help, designed to offer an opportunity for the girls to gain responsibility, maturity, and self-understanding. The girls had resided in the lodge an average of about one year at the time of taking the MMPI. Their mean age was 16.4.

The success group was composed of those girls who were considered to have made an adequate adjustment to the rehabilitation program. They generally controlled their tempers, applied themselves to their studies, and gained increased self-understanding and social acceptability. They were paroled after an average of ten months, and they continued to exhibit adequate conduct. The failure girls were a more diversified group who, for one reason or another, failed to make adequate adjustment to the program. Two girls ran away and were subsequently sent to the State Training School. Three were committed to a state mental hospital. The rest did not fit satisfactorily into the routine of the lodge or, when paroled, got into difficulty and were returned for further work.

The failure group scored higher than the success group on the Sc, Hy, and Pt scales.

Study 50: DELINQUENCY PRONE BOYS (Rempel, 1958). *See Figure 50.*

The subjects were drawn from 1997 ninth-grade boys in the Minneapolis high school system who completed the MMPI in 1948 (see Monachesi, 1953). Their median age was approximately 15 at that time. Invalid profiles (L above 9; F above 14) reduced the sample to 1802.

By checking the city police records and County Probation Office records over the subsequent four years, 351 boys were identified as having committed moderate or severe delinquent acts in the several years after testing.

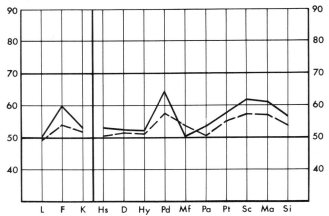

Figure 50. Delinquency Proneness (Male). *Solid Line*: Delinquency Prone Group (N=175). *Broken Line*: Not Delinquency Prone Group (N=175).

The delinquency prone group consisted of a random sample of the 351 boys. The group who were not delinquency prone consisted of a random sample of boys who did not subsequently commit a delinquent act of any kind. They did not differ from the delinquency prone group in educational level, family status, mobility rating, or rent level.

The delinquency prone group scored higher than the group who were not delinquency prone on the Pd, Sc, Ma, and F scales and lower on the Mf scale.

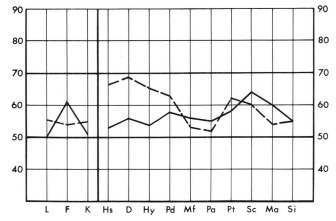

Figure 51a. Adolescent Somatic Disorders (Male). *Solid Line*: Organic Group (N=18, Mean Age 14.9, Age Range 13–16, Mean Education 9.1). *Broken Line*: Functional Group (N=7, Mean Age 14.1, Age Range 13–16, Mean Education 7.7).

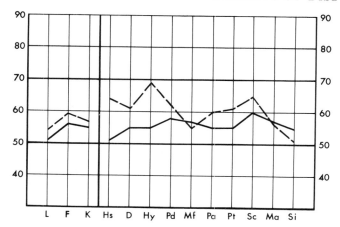

Figure 51b. Adolescent Somatic Disorders (Female). *Solid Line*: Organic (N=26, Mean Age 14.9, Age Range 13–16, Mean Education 8.9). *Broken Line*: Functional (N=22, Mean Age 14.1, Age Range 13–16, Mean Education 8.5).

Study 51: ADOLESCENT SOMATIC DISORDERS

(Stone, Rowley, and MacQueen, 1966). *See Figures 51a–51b.*

The subjects were adolescents who had been referred to the University of Iowa Hospital by local physicians. Most were referred to the Pediatrics Department; none were referred initially to the Psychiatry Department. All patients exhibited symptoms at the time of visiting the hospital and had a single, clear-cut diagnosis. All received T scores below 80 on the L, F, and K scales.

The organic group received diagnoses of convulsive disorder (18), diabetes mellitus (9), heart disease (8), and other (9). The functional group varied in final diagnoses, but in every case it was clear from the final reporting letter to the referring physician that the patient's symptoms were thought to be psychogenic.

For males, the functional group scored higher than the organic group on the Hs scale. For females, the functional group scored higher than the organic group on the Hs, D, Hy, and Pt scales.

Parents of Disturbed Children

Study 52: PARENTS OF DISTURBED CHILDREN (Goodstein and Rowley, 1961). *See Figures 52a–52b.*

The disturbed group consisted of the parents of 50 consecutive cases seen in the Child Psychiatry Service of the State University of Iowa's Psychopathic Hospital. For any case to be included in the study there had to be

available MMPI profiles of both parents, obtained as part of the routine diagnostic procedures. There was no evidence of organicity or mental deficiency for any of the children. Their disturbances were classified as follows: schizophrenic, autistic, or severely schizoid (11); acting-out, delinquent, or antisocial (17); personality trait disturbances such as school problems or enuresis (13); and neurotic problems such as depressions, phobias, and anxieties (9). The control parent group was matched with the disturbed group for age of the child, parental educational level, socioeconomic level, and rural or urban residence. These parents were selected from the pool of MMPI profiles of Iowa parents used in earlier studies. This control group of profiles had been obtained by appeals for volunteers to local PTA's, church groups, and other civic organizations. All these parents had reported that their children were without physical or psychological pathology, and their evaluations were supported by observations of the children in the home by a trained interviewer.

For the mothers, the disturbed group scored higher than the control group on the D, Hy, and Pa scales.

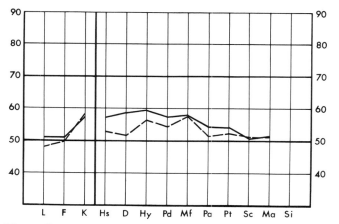

Figure 52a. Fathers of Disturbed Children. *Solid Line*: Disturbed Group (N=50). *Broken Line*: Control Group (N=50).

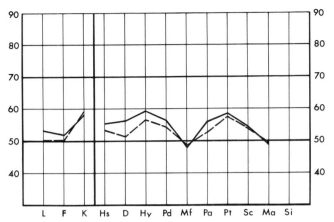

Figure 52b. Mothers of Disturbed Children. *Solid Line*: Disturbed Group (N=50). *Broken Line*: Control Group (N=50).

Twenty-six of the disturbed mothers and 12 of the control mothers had one or more T scores at or above 70; these proportions are significantly different. For the fathers, the disturbed group scored higher than the control group on the Hs and D scales. Twenty-three of the disturbed fathers and 13 of the control fathers had one or more T scores at or above 70; these proportions are significantly different.

Study 53: PARENTS OF DISTURBED CHILDREN (Hanvik and Byrum, 1959). *See Figure 53.*

The subjects consisted of all the parents of children referred to the Washburn Memorial Child Guidance Clinic, Minneapolis, in a two-year period who had taken the MMPI. The test was given routinely at the clinic. The larger number of mothers than fathers resulted part-

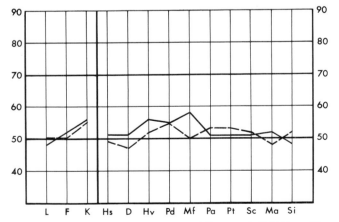

Figure 53. Parents of Disturbed Children. *Solid Line*: Fathers (N=104). *Broken Line*: Mothers (N=158).

ly because a number of the children had no father in the home and partly because some of the fathers did not participate in the clinic treatment program.

Study 54: PARENTS OF DISTURBED CHILDREN (Liverant, 1959). *See Figures 54a–54b.*

The disturbed group consisted of parents (all Caucasian) who had brought a child for evaluation to the Department of Psychiatry at the University of North Carolina Medical School from April 1956 to June 1957, and who took the booklet form of the MMPI as part of the standard diagnostic procedure. In order to be included in the final analysis, both parents had to have taken the

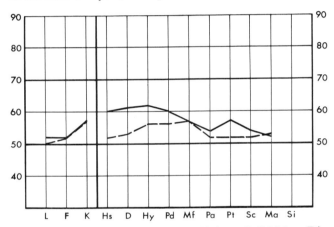

Figure 54a. Fathers of Disturbed Children. *Solid Line*: Disturbed Group (N=49, Mean Age 40, Mean Education 11.6). *Broken Line*: Control Group (N=49, Mean Age 41, Mean Education 12.9).

test and their child had to be judged by the staff to be neither mentally defective nor organically impaired. The disturbed children were classified as schizophrenic (9), acting-out (10), physical complaint (18), and neurotic (12). There were 34 boys and 15 girls, ranging in age from 4 to 17. MMPI differences between parents of the boys and parents of the girls were not large enough to warrant consideration. The control parent data were taken from the population of control parents used by Goodstein and Dahlstrom (1956). These were parents of essentially physically normal, white children with no known behavioral disturbances. They consisted of volunteers from PTA's, church groups, etc., in and around the University of Iowa area. In all cases (as with the experimental sample) both parents were living together at the time of the study. Control parents were matched to disturbed-child parents for age, education, rural or urban

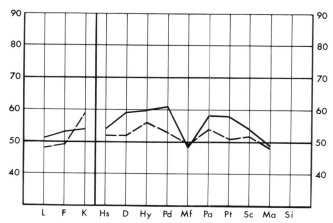

Figure 54b. Mothers of Disturbed Children. *Solid Line*: Disturbed Group (N=49, Mean Age 37, Mean Education 12.4). *Broken Line*: Control Group (N=49, Mean Age 37, Mean Education 13.1).

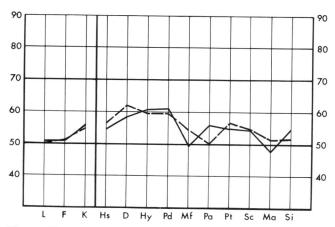

Figure 55. Parents of Disturbed Children. *Solid Line*: Mothers (N=48, Mean Age 37, Mean Education 10.3). *Broken Line*: Fathers (N=32, Mean Age 41, Mean Education 10.1).

residence, and, in the case of fathers, socioeconomic status. Of the disturbed-child group, 82 per cent had urban residences; of the control families, 67 per cent. Over 90 per cent in both groups were Protestant, and they were largely lower-middle-class families.

The disturbed-child fathers scored higher than the control group fathers on the Hs, D, Hy, and Pt scales. Twenty-six fathers in the disturbed-child group had one or more T scores on the nine clinical scales at or above 70, as compared with fifteen of the control group fathers.

The mothers in the disturbed-child group scored higher than the control mothers on the F, D, Hy, Pd, Pa, Pt, and A scales, and lower on the K scale. Twenty-two mothers in the disturbed-child group had one or more T scores on the nine clinical scales at or above 70, as compared with nine of the control group mothers.

Study 55: PARENTS OF DISTURBED CHILDREN (Marks, 1961). *See Figure 55.*

The subjects were the parents of children accepted consecutively for treatment from March to July 1958 at the Amherst H. Wilder Child Guidance Clinic in St. Paul, Minnesota. The mean age of the children was 10 years, and their mean WISC IQ was 101. Seventy-five per cent of the children were males. In almost half the cases, "inability to achieve in school" was listed as a presenting complaint. Occupational distribution of the parents showed some underrepresentation of the lower class.

Comparisons were made with the MMPI standardiza-

tion sample (Hathaway and Briggs, 1957). The mothers of this study scored higher than the standardization sample on the K, Hs, D, Hy, Pd, Pa, Pt, Sc, and Si scales. The fathers of this study scored higher than the standardization sample on the K, Hs, D, Hy, Pd, Mf, Pt, and Sc scales.

Study 56: PARENTS OF DISTURBED CHILDREN (Wolking, Quast, and Lawton, 1966). *See Figure 56.*

The subjects were the parents of children accepted as patients by the Division of Child Psychiatry of the University of Minnesota Medical Center. The MMPI was administered routinely to the parents. The sample included inpatients and outpatients with a wide range of

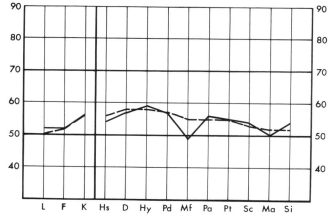

Figure 56. Parents of Disturbed Children. *Solid Line*: Mothers (N=538, Mean Age 37). *Broken Line*: Fathers (N=393, Mean Age 41).

diagnoses. The patients ranged in age from preschool through 15. A case was included if at least one biological parent took the MMPI and the hospital record was reasonably complete. The sample represented more than 90 per cent of the division's total case load over a four-year period. Almost 90 per cent of the child psychiatry patients were living with their biological mothers, but only 73 per cent had their true fathers present in the home. Religious preference and socioeconomic status, as indicated by the Minnesota Scale of Paternal Occupations, did not differ from those of the general population. In light of the general United States census data the sample was overweighted with rural families.

Comparisons were made with the MMPI standardization sample (Hathaway and Briggs, 1957). The mothers of this study scored higher than the standardization sample on all clinical and validity scales except F and Mf. The fathers of this study scored higher than the standardization sample on all clinical and validity scales except L, F, and Si. The samples were broken down into ten subgroups according to the children's diagnoses. For the mothers, there was a striking similarity among the mean profiles for the eight subgroups reported. The fathers' mean profiles were more variable, although the neurotic scales and Pd generally tended to be relatively high, and Ma and Si were usually the low points.

Study 57: PROBLEM BOYS AND THEIR PARENTS (Lauterbach, Vogel, and Hart, 1962). *See Figures 57a–57b.*

The subjects were the father, mother, and problem adolescent son of families referred to an army neuropsychiatric outpatient clinic. Complaints were chronic or acute school underachievement (6), home behavior disorder (4), antisocial acts outside the home reported by school or juvenile authorities (6), emotional immaturity as manifested by enuresis or "acting too young for his age" (3), and severe neurotic symptoms (2). The parents were all native-born white Americans and high school graduates, and the fathers were all career military personnel. Nine of the mothers had attended college, and three had graduated. Fifteen of the fathers had attended college, and eleven had graduated. All sons were living

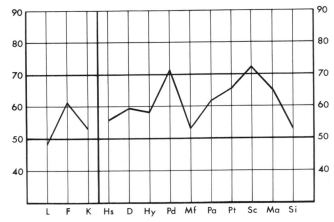

Figure 57a. Problem Boys (N=21, Mean Age 14).

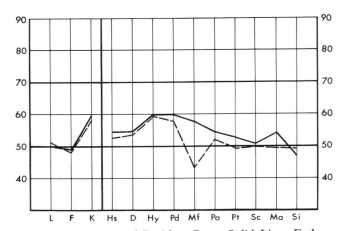

Figure 57b. Parents of Problem Boys. *Solid Line*: Fathers (N=21, Mean Age 42). *Broken Line*: Mothers (N=21, Mean Age 40).

with both biological parents, except for one who had been adopted in the first year of his life. All were enrolled in school; grades ranged from the seventh to the twelfth. Each member of the family was individually given the shortened group form of the MMPI at the first visit to the clinic.

Sons scored higher than their fathers on the F, Pd, Pa, Pt, Sc, Ma, Si, and Mf scales, and lower on the K scale. Sons scored higher than their mothers on the F, Pd, Mf, Pa, Pt, Sc, Ma, and D scales, and lower on the K scale. Fathers and mothers did not differ on any scale except Mf. All family members scored within conventional limits on the validity scales.

Study 58: ARMY PRISONERS (Clark, 1952). *See Figures 58a–58b.*

The subjects were soldiers who had committed serious offenses and had been sentenced to a disciplinary barracks.

Diagnosis, made on the basis of one or more psychiatric interviews, included emotional instability, antisocial personality, and no psychiatric disorder. Subjects in each of the three groups were those for whom MMPI profiles were available.

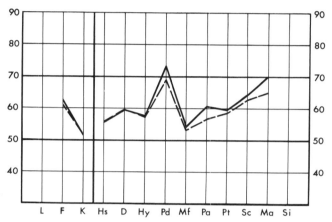

Figure 58a. Army Prisoners with Psychiatric Disorders (Male). *Solid Line*: Antisocial Personality Group (N=43). *Broken Line*: Emotional Instability Group (N=53).

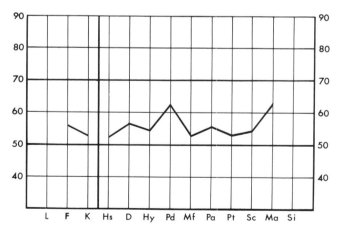

Figure 58b. Army Prisoners with No Psychiatric Disorder (Male, N=40).

The antisocial personality group scored higher than the emotional instability group on the Pd, Pa, and Ma scales, and higher than the no disorder group on the F, Pd, Pa, Pt, Sc, and Ma scales. The emotional instability group scored higher than the no disorder group on the F, Pd, Pt, and Sc scales.

Study 59: ARMY PRISONERS (Kingsley, 1960). *See Figure 59.*

The subjects were enlisted men in the military service.

The prisoner group consisted of 25 offenders who had been diagnosed either antisocial or asocial personality by army psychiatrists and 25 offenders considered by the same psychiatrists to have no psychiatric disorder. The nonprisoner control group were men whose records showed no history of crime, except for minor traffic violations. They were matched individually with the prisoners for education (within two grades) and age (within two years).

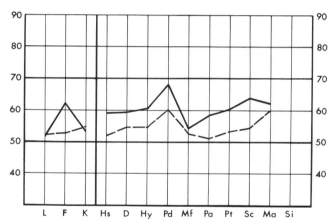

Figure 59. Army Prisoners (Male). *Solid Line*: Prisoners (N=50). *Broken Line*: Nonprisoners (N=50).

The prisoners scored higher than the nonprisoners on the F, Hs, Hy, Pd, Pa, Pt, and Sc scales. No differences were found between the groups on Welsh's anxiety index (AI) or internalization ratio (IR). There were no MMPI differences between the 25 prisoners diagnosed antisocial or asocial and the 25 prisoners considered to have no psychiatric disorder.

Study 60: CRIMINALS CLASSIFIED BY OFFENSE (Panton, 1959). *See Figures 60a–60c.*

The subjects were 1313 prisoners at the Central Prison in North Carolina tested during 1955–56. Profiles

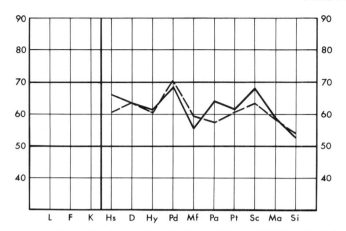

Figure 60a. Criminals Classified by Offense (Male). *Solid Line*: Aggravated Sex Group (N=63). *Broken Line*: Sex Perversive Group (N=73).

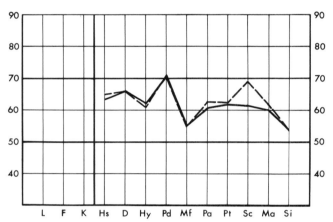

Figure 60b. Criminals Classified by Offense (Male). *Solid Line*: White-Collar Group (N=233). *Broken Line*: Aggravated Assault Group (N=157).

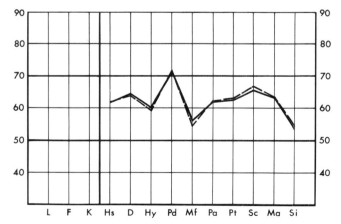

Figure 60c. Criminals Classified by Offense (Male). *Solid Line*: Robbery-Burglary Group (N=219). *Broken Line*: Property Theft Group (N=568).

were rejected if they included an L or K scale score above 70 or an F scale score above 80. All subjects had IQ scores above 80.

The prisoners were divided into subgroups according to the type of criminal activity in which they had been involved: white collar (forgery, embezzlement, false pretense, fraud, etc.); aggravated assault (murder, assault, secret assault, etc.); robbery-burglary (house burglary, store robbery, highway robbery, etc.); property theft (larceny, larceny of automobile, etc.); aggravated sex (rape, assault with intent to commit rape, etc.); sex perversive (homosexual and heterosexual).

The white collar group scored higher than the total sample on the Hy scale, and lower on the Sc and Ma scales. The aggravated assault group scored higher than the total sample on the Sc scale. The robbery-burglary group did not differ from the total sample on any scale. The property theft group scored higher than the total sample on the Sc and Ma scales and lower on the Hy scale. The aggravated sex group scored lower than the total sample on the Ma scale. The sex perversive group scored higher than the total sample on the Mf scale and lower on the Pa, Pt, and Ma scales.

Study 61: GROUP THERAPY WITH SEX OFFENDERS (Cabeen and Coleman, 1961). *See Figure 61.*

The subjects were 120 sex offenders who had been committed to Metropolitan State Hospital by the California courts. They had been arrested for sex offenses and adjudged to be "sexual psychopaths," as defined by law, after initial examination by at least two psychiatrists and a 90-day observation period in the state hospital. The psychiatric diagnosis was "psychopath" for 69 subjects and "neurotic" for 51. The great majority of cases involved molestation of children or minors. Offenses against adults fell chiefly in the category of exhibitionism. Eighty subjects had committed offenses against female sex objects, and 40 against male sex objects. Sixty-five were first arrests and 54 were repeaters. Organics, seniles, mental defectives, and possible psychotics were excluded. All were judged to be potentially treatable.

Subjects were tested before therapy and after therapy. The therapy program involved three complementary approaches: development of a "therapeutic community" on each ward, formal group psychotherapy, and adjunctive therapy such as occupational and recreational therapy.

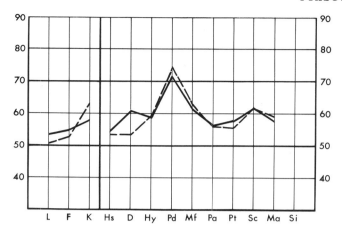

Figure 61. Group Therapy with Sex Offenders (Male, N= 120, Mean Age 35, Age Range 17–67, Mean IQ 109). *Solid Line*: Pre-Therapy Tests. *Broken Line*: Post-Therapy Tests.

The mean number of group therapy sessions was 34 (range 1–52).

The pre-therapy scores were higher than the post-therapy scores on the D scale and the sexual deviation scale of Marsh, Hilliard, and Liechti (1955), and lower on the K scale.

Study 62: HABITUAL AND NONHABITUAL CRIMINALS (Panton, 1962a). *See Figure 62.*

The subjects were drawn from the files of the North Carolina Prison Reception Center.

The habitual criminal group consisted of those men aged 40 or over who had served three or more felon sentences before their current incarceration. The nonhabit-

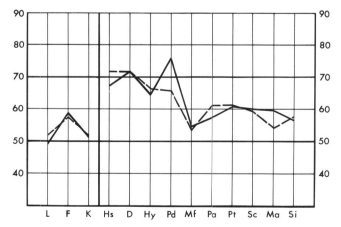

Figure 62. Habitual and Nonhabitual Criminals (Male). *Solid Line*: Habitual Group (N=50, Mean Age 46, Mean IQ 101). *Broken Line*: Nonhabitual Group (N=50, Mean Age 47, Mean IQ 97).

ual criminal group were first offenders aged 40 and over who had spent 20 years or more gainfully employed before their first imprisonment. They were matched with the habitual criminals on age and IQ. Cases involving physical or mental illness were excluded from both samples.

The habitual criminals scored significantly higher than the nonhabituals on the Pd and Ma scales, and also on two special scales (Rc and Ap) which had been previously derived for specific use with prison populations.

Study 63: HOMOSEXUAL AND HETEROSEXUAL PRISONERS (Miller and Hannum, 1963). *See Figure 63.*

The subjects were prisoners of the Iowa State Women's Reformatory at Rockwell City.

The homosexual group met all the following criteria: (a) discovery, through a counseling relationship, of participation in overt homosexual acts while incarcerated;

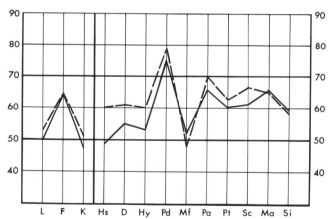

Figure 63. Homosexual and Heterosexual Prisoners (Female). *Solid Line*: Homosexuals (N=17). *Broken Line*: Heterosexuals (N=17).

(b) reports of other prisoners and prison personnel about the homosexual behavior of the persons in question; and (c) admission, within a counseling relationship, of actively seeking homosexual experiences during incarceration. The heterosexual group met all the following criteria: (a) a profession of no homosexual inclination; (b) no evidence in prison records of any homosexual activities, and (c) no report by fellow prisoners or prison personnel of ever participating in overt homosexual behavior while incarcerated.

Comparison of the distribution of the highest and lowest scores on each scale by chi-square tests suggested that the heterosexual group had higher scores than the homosexual group on the Hs scale and lower scores on the Mf scale.

Study 64: LITERATE AND SEMILITERATE PRISONERS (Wolf, Freinek, and Shaffer, 1964). *See Figure 64.*

The subjects were penitentiary inmates, to whom the MMPI was administered in oral form. Their median age was 19. (Further data on these two groups are presented in Study 103.)

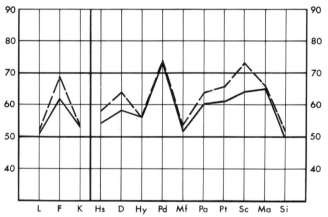

Figure 64. Literate and Semiliterate Prisoners (Male). *Solid Line:* Literates (N=120). *Broken Line:* Semiliterates (N=120).

The literate group had a reading level of sixth grade and above. The semiliterate group had a reading level below sixth grade.

The semiliterate group scored higher than the literate group on the F, Hs, D, Pa, Pt, and Sc scales. It should be noted that these statistical comparisons were made on profiles which were *not* corrected for K, and are thus only approximate for the K-corrected scales reported here.

Study 65: SELF-MUTILATOR PRISONERS (Panton, 1962b). *See Figures 65a–65b.*

The subjects were prisoners at the Central Prison, North Carolina. Length of sentence ranged from 1 to 40 years.

The self-mutilation group consisted of 37 carefully documented case histories of self-mutilation. All these prisoners had histories of poor prison adjustment,

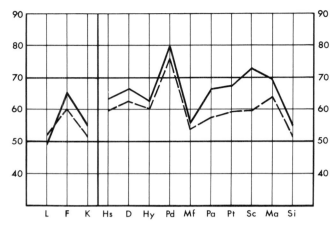

Figure 65a. Self-Mutilator Prisoners (Male). *Solid Line:* Self-Mutilation Group (N=37, Mean Age 24, Mean IQ 97, Mean Education 8.2). *Broken Line:* Matched Control Group (N=37, Mean Age 24, Mean IQ 99, Mean Education 7.8).

marked by numerous displays of physical violence before resort to self-injury. None of the group claimed they were actually trying to destroy themselves, nor did the psychiatric examinations reveal any suicidal intentions. Mutilation by laceration of the arms, hands, legs, and feet occurred in 34 cases, laceration of the chest and abdomen in 2 cases; and 1 case resorted to pouring caustic potash in superficial lacerations on the arms and legs. The matched control group was paired with the self-mutilators in number and type of infractions and degree of exposure to custodial stress and pressure. The criminal records of the self-mutilators and the matched controls revealed similar criminal histories, involving physical violence (murder, assault, robbery by force, etc.). The groups were also matched for IQ (Beta), education, and

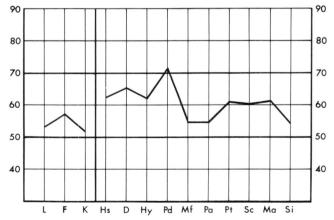

Figure 65b. Model Prisoner Control Group (Male, N=37, Mean Age 26, Mean IQ 99, Mean Education 8.6).

educational achievement level on the Wide Range Achievement Test. The model prisoner control group was also used for comparison. Their crimes for the most part had been limited to nonviolent, white-collar criminal activity, such as fraud, forgery, and embezzlement. They appeared to continue the same pattern of nonviolence during confinement as they displayed in their criminal histories. They were matched with the other two groups on age, IQ, education, and educational achievement level.

The self-mutilators scored higher than the matched controls on the F, Pa, Pt, Sc, and Ma scales. The self-mutilators scored higher than the model prisoners on the F, Pd, Pa, Pt, Sc, and Ma scales. The matched controls and the model prisoners did not differ on any of the scales.

Study 66: SEX OFFENDERS (Swenson and Grimes, 1958). *See Figure 66.*

The subjects were 45 male sex offenders in the state of Minnesota who were hospitalized for pre-sentence investigation between 1953 and 1956. The majority had been convicted of indecent assault, and the remaining offenses included sodomy, rape, incest, and indecent exposure. Approximately half of the subjects had histories of committing major felonies. About half of the subjects were married and had been living with their wives at the time of the offense. More than half were above the average range in intelligence. The majority of the victims were female, almost half of whom were between the ages of seven and ten.

Study 67: SEX OFFENDERS (Wattron, 1958). *See Figure 67.*

The subjects were convicted sex offenders in a Texas state prison who had taken the MMPI as part of their classification procedure. There were 7 Latin-Americans, 10 Negroes, and 43 Caucasians roughly approximating the ratio of these groups in the institution. Otis IQ scores were available. The subjects had been convicted of the following charges: rape and assault to rape (34), sodomy (14), indecent exposure (3), fondling (5), and bigamy with chaotic sexual patterning (4). There were no MMPI differences among these subcategories.

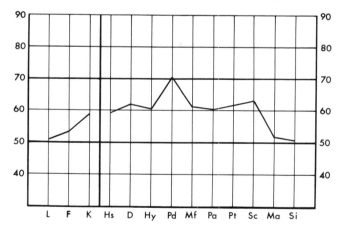

Figure 66. Sex Offenders (Male, N=45, Mean Age 37, Age Range 21–67, Mean IQ 109).

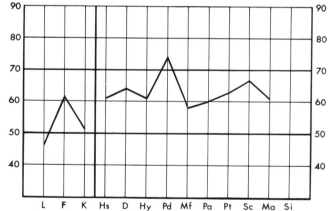

Figure 67. Sex Offenders (Male, N=60, Mean Age 31, Age Range 18–58, Mean IQ 92, IQ Range 70–121).

Student and Occupational Groups

Study 68: ACTORS (Taft, 1961). *See Figures 68a–68b.*

Those in the actor group were all professionally employed in the theater, and were drawn mostly from companies on tour in Perth, Australia. About 56 per cent of those approached volunteered to take part in a psychological study of the theatrical profession, of which ad-

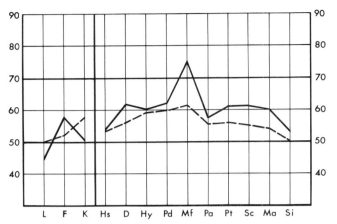

Figure 68a. Actors and Students (Male). *Solid Line*: Actors (N=46, Mean IQ approx. 112). *Broken Line*: Students (N= 25, Mean IQ approx. 120).

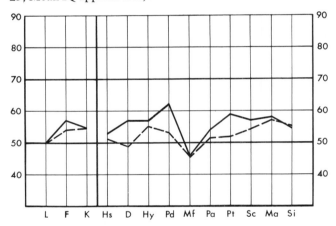

Figure 68b. Actors and Students (Female). *Solid Line*: Actors (N=28, Mean IQ approx. 112). *Broken Line*: Students (N=25, Mean IQ approx. 120).

ministration of the MMPI was one aspect. The population, which included actors, singers, dancers, stage directors, and writer-producers, included "any person who, at the time of interview, or within the previous year, was deriving the major part of his/her livelihood from theatrical stage performances." About half were actors by main occupation. The mean number of years in the theater was 14 (median 7). Students drawn from first-year psychology courses were matched with the actors for age (separately by sex). Socioeconomic status was considered to be equivalent. None of the students were professional actors.

The male actors scored higher than the male students on the F, D, Mf, Pt, Sc, Ma, and A scales and lower on the L, K, and Es scales. The female actors scored higher than the female students on the D, Pd, and Pt scales.

Study 69: ART STUDENTS (Spiaggia, 1950). *See Figure 69.*

The art students were all volunteers who had attended a recognized art school in New York City (excluding commercial-art schools) for at least two years, and who intended to make art work their vocation. They were 18 or older. The miscellaneous normal group was composed

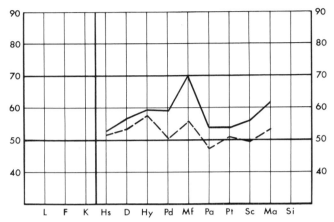

Figure 69. Art Students and Normals (Male). *Solid Line*: Art Students (N=50, Mean Age 25, Mean IQ 112). *Broken Line*: Miscellaneous Normals (N=50, Mean Age 25, Mean IQ 113).

of subjects who were not art students, selected randomly from the general population in New York City and in Rockland and Orange Counties of New York State. The sample included hospital attendants, automobile mechanics, electricians, shoemakers, chauffeurs, teachers, accountants, and graduate students. They were individually matched with the art students on the basis of chronological age and Otis IQ.

The art students scored higher than the miscellaneous group on the D, Pd, Mf, Pa, Pt, Sc, and Ma scales.

Study 70: COLLEGE MAJOR GROUPS (Norman and Redlo, 1952). *See Figures 70a–70c.*

The subjects were seniors and graduate students at the University of New Mexico. They were grouped by logical relationships into the six categories referred to below. (A seventh category, geology, was included in the original study.)

The psychology-sociology group scored lower than the total combined group on the Pa scale. The anthropology group did not differ from the total group on any of the scales. The mathematics-chemistry-physics group scored lower than the total group on the Sc scale. The engineer-

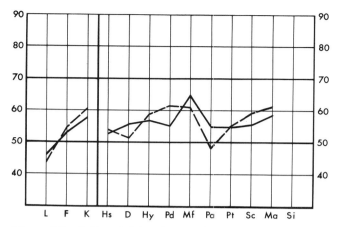

Figure 70a. College Major Groups (Male). *Solid Line*: Anthropology Group (N=22). *Broken Line*: Psychology-Sociology Group (N=20).

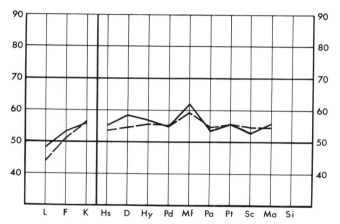

Figure 70b. College Major Groups (Male). *Solid Line*: Mathematics-Chemistry-Physics Group (N=18). *Broken Line*: Engineering Group (N=29).

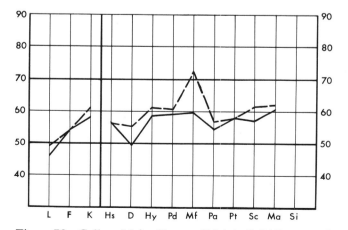

Figure 70c. College Major Groups (Male). *Solid Line*: Business Administration Group (N=23). *Broken Line*: Art-Music Group (N=17).

ing group scored lower than the total group on the F, Mf, and Ma scales. The business administration group scored lower than the total group on the D scale. The art-music group scored higher than the total group on the L and Mf scales.

Study 71: GIFTED ADOLESCENTS (Kennedy, 1962). *See Figure 71.*

The subjects were mathematically gifted adolescent students who attended the summer math institute at Florida State University. The students came from high schools in most of the 50 states and were on campus for

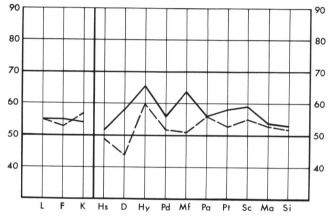

Figure 71. Gifted Adolescents. *Solid Line*: Boys (N=79, Mean IQ 136). *Broken Line*: Girls (N=21, Mean IQ 132).

six weeks of intensive and extensive exposure to higher mathematics. Their mean age was 17.4. The students were exceptional on two counts: their high intellectual ability and their high productivity, from the point of view of both a superior general scholastic record and special mathematical achievement. There were no MMPI validity T scores above 70.

Study 72: GRADUATES AND NONGRADUATES (Drasgow and McKenzie, 1958). *See Figure 72.*

The subjects were drawn sequentially from the alphabetically arranged folders of students in the University of Buffalo's Liberal Arts College. The students had taken the MMPI as entering freshmen.

The graduates consisted of those who had since successfully graduated from the college. The nongraduates had one year or less of college work on record. Since everyone had begun 10 years previously, the possibility of temporary withdrawal was lessened.

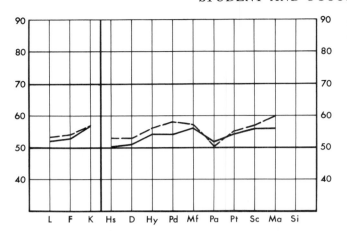

Figure 72. Graduates and Nongraduates (Male and Female). *Solid Line*: Graduates (N=50). *Broken Line*: Nongraduates (N=50).

The nongraduates scored higher than the graduates on the Pd and Ma scales.

Study 73: LUTHERAN MINISTERS (Lucero and Currens, 1964). *See Figure 73.*

The subjects were Lutheran ministers who were tested on the first day (pre-training) and again on the last day (post-training) of a two-week clinical pastoral training program. The program followed national standards with the addition of personal psychotherapy, administered through psychodrama.

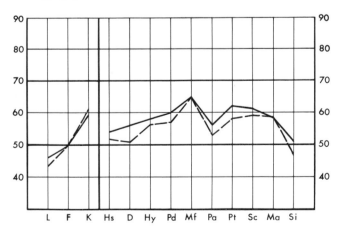

Figure 73. Lutheran Ministers (Male, N=37). *Solid Line*: Pre-Training Tests. *Broken Line*: Post-Training Tests.

The scores for the pre-training test were higher than the post-training test on the L, K, Hs, D, Pt, Sc, and Si scales.

Study 74: MEDICAL STUDENTS (Schofield, 1953). *See Figure 74.*

The subjects were University of Minnesota medical students, who took the MMPI in their freshman year and again in their junior year.

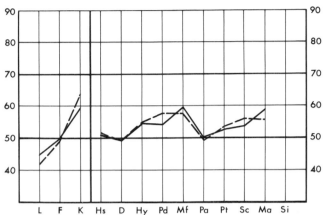

Figure 74. Medical Students (Male, N=83). *Solid Line*: Tests as Freshmen. *Broken Line*: Tests as Juniors.

The scores for the group as freshmen were higher than those for the group as juniors on the L, F, Mf, and Ma scales, and lower on the K and Pd scales.

Study 75: NINTH-GRADE STUDENTS (Hathaway and Monachesi, 1963). *See Figure 75.*

The subjects were drawn from 92 schools in 82 communities, in 47 of Minnesota's 87 counties. Schools were selected as much as possible to represent Minnesota's diverse economic and geographic areas. The sample in-

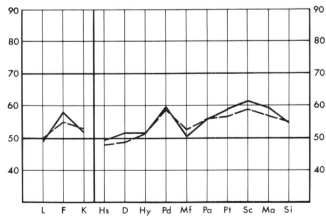

Figure 75. Ninth-Grade Students. *Solid Line*: Boys (N=4944, Mean Age 14.6). *Broken Line*: Girls (N=5207, Mean Age 14.4).

cluded 28 per cent of the entire ninth-grade public school population in Minneapolis and St. Paul, 36 per cent of all ninth grades outside the Twin City public school systems, and 101 boys and girls from Roman Catholic parochial schools. All profiles included had a raw score below 10 on the L scale and below 16 on the F scale.

Study 76: SEMINARY STUDENTS (Baer and Moynihan, 1964). *See Figure 76.*

The subjects were white, American-born, college-age men accepted into the New England Province of the Society of Jesus in the years 1956–61.

The stayers consisted of those subjects who were still members of the Society after several years. The leavers consisted of those who subsequently left the Society.

The stayers scored lower than the leavers on the K scale. (Stayers also achieved higher K-uncorrected scores on the Sc scale.) A stepwise linear discriminant-function analysis failed on cross-validation to differentiate stayers and leavers with better than chance accuracy.

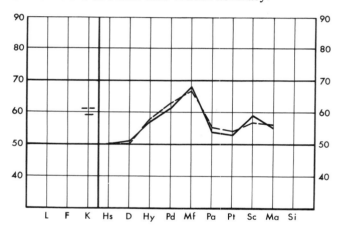

Figure 76. Seminary Students (Male). *Solid Line:* Stayers (N=140). *Broken Line:* Leavers (N=62).

Study 77: SEMINARY STUDENTS (Bier, 1948). *See Figure 77.*

The seminary students were drawn from diocesan seminaries and from three religious orders. They were all major seminarians, engaged in the study of either phi-

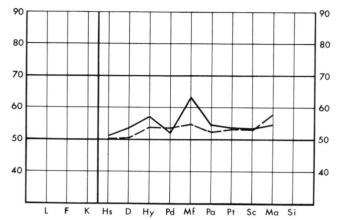

Figure 77. Seminary and College Students (Male). *Solid Line:* Seminary Group (N=171, Mean Age 26). *Broken Line:* College Group (N=369, Mean Age 18). Note: These profiles are not K-corrected.

losophy or theology in preparation for the Catholic priesthood. They were geographically well distributed, being drawn from the East, the Midwest, and the Far West. Three respondents were rejected from the sample on the basis of their scores on the validity scales. The college control group was composed of college students who were both Catholic and unmarried. Seventeen students were rejected from the sample on the basis of their scores on the validity scales.

Comparisons between the groups were made using a covariance procedure to control for the effect of age differences. The seminary group scored higher than the college control group on the Mf scale.

Race and Culture

Study 78: AUSTRALIAN AND UNITED STATES COLLEGE STUDENTS (Taft, 1957). *See Figures 78a–78b.*

The Australian subjects were first-year psychology students at the University of Western Australia. Those

not educated in Britain or Australia were eliminated. The test was taken anonymously as part of a laboratory training exercise. The mean age, especially of the males, was somewhat high due to the inclusion of part-time students. The United States group was drawn from a

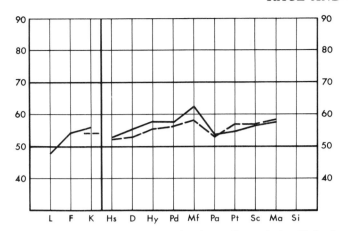

Figure 78a. College Students in Australia and the United States (Male). *Solid Line*: Australians (N=65, Mean Age 26.6, Mean IQ approx. 124). *Broken Line*: Americans (N= 5742).

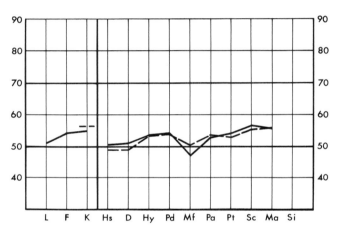

Figure 78b. College Students in Australia and the United States (Female). *Solid Line*: Australians (N=65, Mean Age 21, Mean IQ approx. 124). *Broken Line*: Americans (N= 5014).

combination of 10 studies of male college undergraduates, 9 of which were integrated by Goodstein (1954), and 15 studies of female undergraduates from various regions of the United States (Black, 1956).

Among the males the Australian group scored higher than the United States group on the Mf scale. The Australians also obtained more abnormal scores (T above 70) on the Hy, Pd, Mf, and Pa scales. A comparison of 30 subjects from the Australian sample (in the age range 17–24) showed that these differences could not be attributed to an age discrepancy. Among the females the Australian group scored lower than the United States group on the Mf scale. There were no differences between the groups in the proportion of abnormal scores on any scale.

Study 79: GERMAN TRANSLATION (Sundberg, 1956). *See Figures 79a–79b.*

The German group consisted of students at the International Holiday Course at the University of Marburg, in the summer of 1948, who volunteered or were persuaded to take the test anonymously. Their previous university attendance averaged 5 semesters (range 0–11). This average would roughly correspond to the American senior year or first graduate year, since German schools are so organized that the student enters a university at a later educational stage. About half of the German stu-

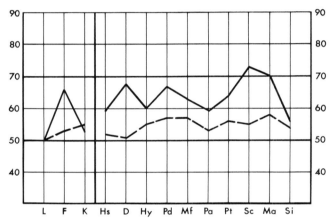

Figure 79a. College Students in Germany and the United States (Male). *Solid Line*: Germans (N=60). *Broken Line*: Americans (N=1422).

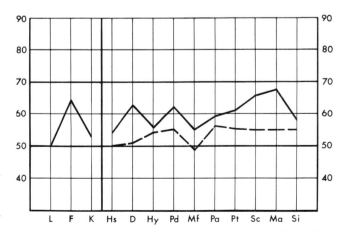

Figure 79b. College Students in Germany and the United States (Female). *Solid Line*: Germans (N=51). *Broken Line*: Americans (N=760).

dents were from Marburg University and the rest from other western zone universities. Forty per cent were students in the faculty of philosophy (corresponding roughly to the American liberal arts college), 20 per cent in law, 12 per cent in medicine, and 6 per cent in theology. The original form of the German translation of the MMPI was developed in 1948, and included 399 items, being those required for the validity scales, the usual clinical scales, and the Si scale. The translation was done with the assistance of two native German-speaking students who had studied English several years. It was checked by a professor of English at the University of Marburg. The United States group consisted of entering freshman at the University of Wisconsin in 1948.

The German group of males scored higher than the United States group of males on all scales except K. The German group of females scored higher than the United States group of females on all scales except L and Hy.

It is pointed out that the usual interpretations applied to the United States profiles obviously do not apply to the German ones.

Study 80: ITALIAN AND UNITED STATES MEN (Rosen and Rizzo, 1961). *See Figures 80a–80b.*

These data were gathered in preliminary standardization of an Italian translation of the MMPI. Since the translation of some of the items was subsequently changed as a result of the study, the data are not identical with those derived from the final version of the MMPI now in use in Italy.

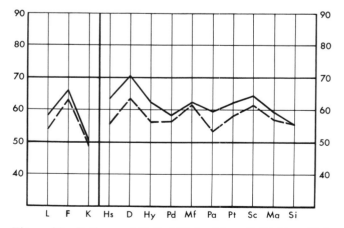

Figure 80a. Italian and United States Men. *Solid Line*: Italian Southern Group (N=45). *Broken Line*: Italian Central Group (N=51).

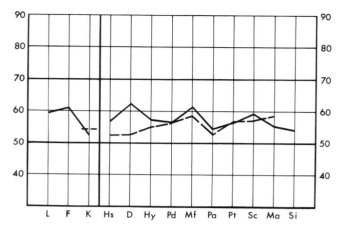

Figure 80b. Italian and United States Men. *Solid Line*: Italian Northern Group (N=43). *Broken Line*: U.S. College Group (N=5035).

The Italian subjects were army enlisted men in the early stages of basic training. All had had 12 years of schooling. They were grouped according to residence in northern, central, or southern Italy. The geographic regions in Italy differ from each other in many ways. Northern Italy is ahead of the central and southern regions in industrialization, per capita income, standards of living, and communication facilities, and it has the densest population. Southern Italy is least industrialized and has the lowest living standards. Sociological and cultural differences between central and southern Italy are somewhat greater than between the northern and central areas. The United States college scores represent the medians of a set of student means compiled by Goodstein (1954) from several sources.

The northern Italian group scored higher than the United States college group on the D and Hs scales and lower on the Ma scale. The central Italian group scored higher than the United States college group on the Hs, D, Hy, Mf, Pa, Sc, and Pt scales and lower on the K scale.

Study 81: ITALIAN AND UNITED STATES WOMEN (Rosen and Rizzo, 1961). *See Figure 81.*

These data were gathered in preliminary standardization of an Italian translation of the MMPI. Since the translation of some of the items was subsequently changed as a result of the study, the data are not identical with those derived from the final version of the MMPI now in use in Italy.

The Italian sample consisted of 50 female university

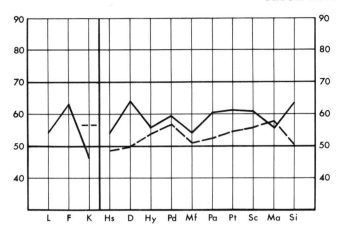

Figure 81. Italian and United States Women. *Solid Line*: Italian College Group (N=50). *Broken Line*: U.S. College Group (N=151).

students, the majority from central Italy. The United States subjects consisted of a comparable group of college females.

The Italian women scored higher than the United States women on the Hs, D, Pa, Pt, Sc, Si, and Mf scales and lower on the K scale.

Study 82: NEGRO AND WHITE STUDENTS (Ball, 1960). *See Figures 82a–82b.*

The subjects were from the ninth grade in two integrated public schools in Kentucky. They constituted the entire ninth grade in attendance at the time the test was administered, except for 24 subjects who completed invalid profiles. The Negro and white students attended

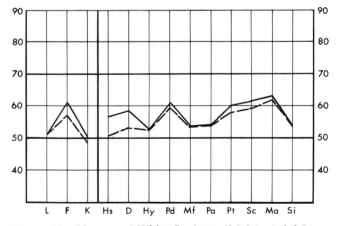

Figure 82a. Negro and White Students (Male). *Solid Line*: Negroes (N=14, Mean Age 15, Mean IQ approx. 96). *Broken Line*: Whites (N=81, Mean Age 15, Mean IQ approx. 104).

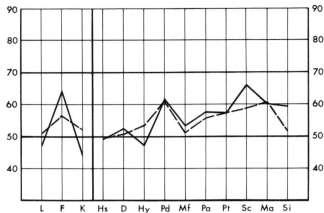

Figure 82b. Negro and White Students (Female). *Solid Line*: Negroes (N=17, Mean Age 14, Mean IQ approx. 94). *Broken Line*: Whites (N=88, Mean Age 15, Mean IQ approx. 105).

the same classes and lived in the same school districts. A greater percentage of the Negroes (36 vs. 9 for boys; 29 vs. 18 for girls) came from broken homes. In addition, a significantly greater percentage of the Negroes (86 vs. 18 for boys; 65 vs. 14 for girls) came from the lowest two of the seven classes on the Minnesota Parental Occupation scale, while the whites were predominantly from higher status families. The Negroes had grade averages below those of the whites, but the groups did not differ significantly in the percentage of educationally retarded students.

Among the boys, the Negroes scored higher than the whites on the Hs scale. Among the girls, the Negroes scored higher than the whites on the F, Si, and Sc scales and lower on the K and Hy scales. The percentage of students with one or more scales at or above a T score of 70 did not differ among the four groups.

Study 83: NEGRO AND WHITE STUDENTS (Butcher, Ball, and Ray, 1964). *See Figures 83a–83d.*

The subjects were college students in North Carolina. All were born and educated in the state, and were currently enrolled in introductory psychology courses. Invalid profiles (L above 70, F above 80, or K above 70) were eliminated. Family income and occupation data were collected, and socioeconomic level was determined from a modified form of Warner's Occupational Index. Mean MMPI profiles were calculated for entire groups (N = 50) and also for subgroups (N = 26) matched for socioeconomic level.

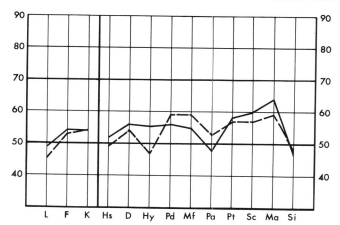

Figure 83a. Negro and White Students (Male). *Solid Line*: Negroes (N=50, Age Range 19–22). *Broken Line*: Whites (N=50, Age Range 19–22).

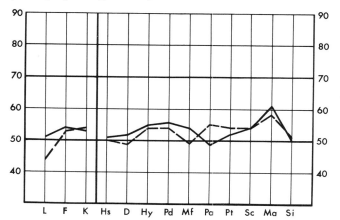

Figure 83b. Negro and White Students (Female). *Solid Line*: Negroes (N=50, Age Range 19–22). *Broken Line*: Whites (N=50, Age Range 19–22).

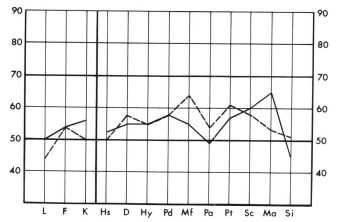

Figure 83c. Negro and White Students Matched for Socio-economic Level (Male). *Solid Line*: Negroes (N=26, Age Range 19–22). *Broken Line*: Whites (N=26, Age Range 19–22).

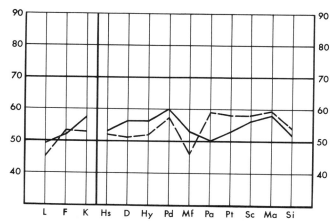

Figure 83d. Negro and White Students Matched for Socio-economic Level (Female). *Solid Line*: Negroes (N=16, Age Range 19–22). *Broken Line*: Whites (N=16, Age Range 19–22).

The Negro subjects were students at North Carolina College. The white subjects were students at the University of North Carolina.

Comparison of the unmatched groups showed that the Negro males scored higher than the white males on the L and Ma scales and lower on the Pa and Es scales; and that the Negro females scored higher than the white females on the L and Mf scales and lower on the Pa and R scales. Comparison of subgroups matched for socioeconomic level showed that the Negro males scored higher than the white males on the L, K, Ma, and Es scales and lower on the Mf, Pa, Pt, Si, and A scales; and that the Negro females scored higher than the white females on the L and Mf scales and lower on the Pa scale. It should be noted that all statistical comparisons were made on profiles which were *not* corrected for K, and are thus only approximate for the K-corrected scales reported here.

Study 84: NEGRO AND WHITE MEDICAL PATIENTS (Hokanson and Calden, 1960). *See Figure 84.*

The subjects were male tuberculosis patients admitted consecutively to the VA Hospital in Madison, Wisconsin, during a six-month period. The individual form of the MMPI was administered during their first month of hospitalization as part of a study of the relationship of personality and body type to tuberculosis. Subjects were rejected if they had a T score above 70 on the L or K scales, or above 80 on the F scale. Both groups came from predominantly northern working-class settings, and

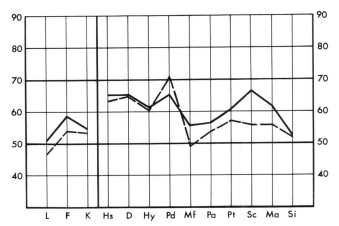

Figure 84. Negro and White Medical Patients (Male). *Solid Line*: Negroes (N=34, Mean Age 32). *Broken Line*: Whites (N=34, Mean Age 35).

a chi-square test showed no difference between them with respect to white collar versus manual labor types of occupations.

The Negro group scored higher than the white group on the L, F, Mf, Sc, and Ma scales and lower on the Pd scale.

Study 85: NEGRO AND WHITE PSYCHIATRIC PATIENTS (Miller, Wertz, and Counts, 1961). *See Figure 85.*

The subjects were applicants for treatment at a VA mental hygiene clinic. There were no significant differences between the groups in age, employment status, or education. Both groups were well above the average for

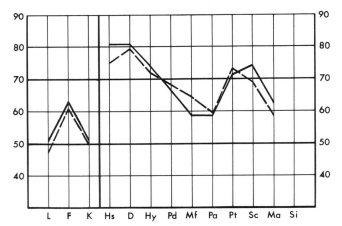

Figure 85. Negro and White Psychiatric Patients (Male). *Solid Line*: Negroes (N=100). *Broken Line*: Whites (N=100).

the general population in education. Thirty-nine per cent of the Negroes were in the unskilled labor category, while only 8 per cent of the whites were in this group.

The Negro group scored higher than the white group on the L, Hs, and Ma scales and lower on the Mf scale.

Study 86: NEGRO AND WHITE SOCIOECONOMIC DIFFERENCES (McDonald and Gynther, 1963). *See Figures 86a–86d.*

The subjects were drawn from a group consisting of 354 (196 female and 158 male) Negro and 263 (132 female and 131 male) white high school seniors who constituted consecutive graduating classes (1961 and 1962) of

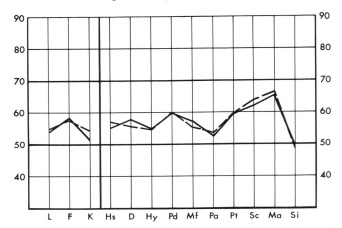

Figure 86a. Negro Socioeconomic Status (Male). *Solid Line*: High-Status Group (N=30, Age Range 16–19). *Broken Line*: Low-Status Group (N=30, Age Range 16–19).

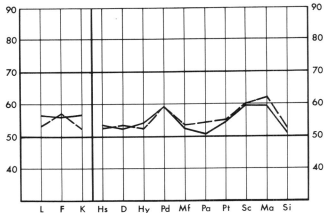

Figure 86b. Negro Socioeconomic Status (Female). *Solid Line*: High-Status Group (N=30, Age Range 16–19). *Broken Line*: Low-Status Group (N=30, Age Range 16–19).

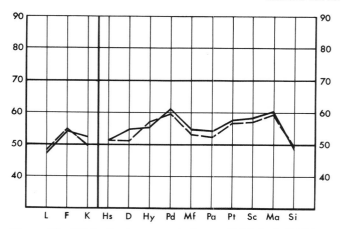

Figure 86c. White Socioeconomic Status (Male). *Solid Line*: High-Status Group (N=30, Age Range 16–19). *Broken Line*: Low-Status Group (N=30, Age Range 16–19).

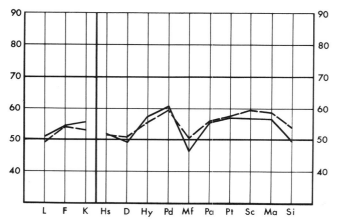

Figure 86d. White Socioeconomic Status (Female). *Solid Line*: High-Status Group (N=30, Age Range 16–19). *Broken Line*: Low-Status Group (N=30, Age Range 16–19).

urban segregated southern high schools. There were no mean age differences by sex or race. The MMPI was administered by school counselors during special group testing periods. Each student was also instructed to list the occupational status and job title, if known, of both parents on a form provided for this purpose. Inspection of the MMPI answer sheets revealed no invalid records either through inability to understand the instructions or through omission of an excessive number of items. Tests were not discarded because of high L or F scores. Subjects were randomly deleted until the subgroups were all of a size equal to the smallest subgroup (i.e., 30).

The high-status groups were those whose parents were rated 1 or 2 on Schneider and Lysgaard's (1953) occupational classification scheme. These groups comprised

(1) independent or professional occupations; and (2) dependent occupations involving skill and supervision or manipulation of others (including supervisors, foremen, public officials, sales workers). In the minority of cases where the father's occupation was unclassifiable, the maternal occupational status was used for classification purposes. Two judges, the junior author and a second clinical psychologist, independently rated the maternal and paternal occupations in terms of the various classifications. The low-status groups were those whose parents were rated 4 on the Schneider-Lysgaard scheme, indicating dependent occupations involving little skill and little supervision or manipulation of others. Data presented

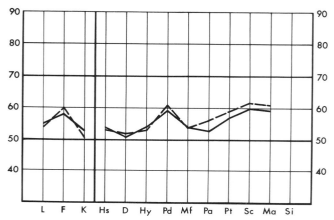

Figure 87a. Social Class (Male). *Solid Line*: Higher Socioeconomic Group (N=123, Mean Age 15.9). *Broken Line*: Lower Socioeconomic Group (N=56, Mean Age 16.1, Mean IQ 109).

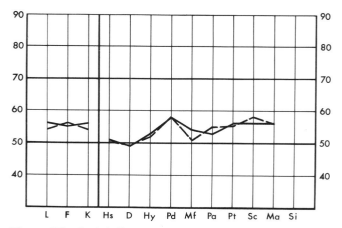

Figure 87b. Social Class (Female). *Solid Line*: Higher Socioeconomic Group (N=79, Mean Age 16.4). *Broken Line*: Lower Socioeconomic Group (N=223, Mean Age 16.0, Mean IQ 108).

for subjects in occupational group 3 are omitted in the present summary.

Study 87: SOCIAL CLASS (Monachesi, 1953). *See Figures 87a–87b.*

The higher socioeconomic class sample, or academy group, was drawn from students in a denominational academy located in one of the better residential sections of Minneapolis. Tuition was high enough to exclude lower income classes. The majority of paternal occupations (70–80 per cent) were classed as professional or skilled.

The lower socioeconomic class sample was drawn from the Boy Scouts, Girl Scouts, Girl Reserves, boys in a settlement house recreational club, boys from a Hi-Y group, and boys and girls from two high school classes. The occupations of 24 per cent of the fathers of the lower socioeconomic class sample were classed as professional or skilled.

The higher socioeconomic boys scored higher than the lower socioeconomic boys on the L scale. The higher socioeconomic girls scored higher than the lower socioeconomic girls on the L and Mf scales and lower on the Pa scale.

Miscellaneous Groups

Study 88: EFFECT OF AGE (Calden and Hokanson, 1959). *See Figure 88.*

The subjects were approximately 90 per cent of the male tuberculosis patients in the relevant age groups who were admitted consecutively to the VA Hospital, Madison, Wisconsin, during a six-month period. The individual form of the MMPI was administered during their first month of hospitalization. Records with L or K scale scores above 70 or an F scale score above 80 were rejected. (Data for three additional age groups are presented in the original study.)

Statistical comparisons over the five age groups originally presented indicated that the Hs, D, and Si scale scores increased with age.

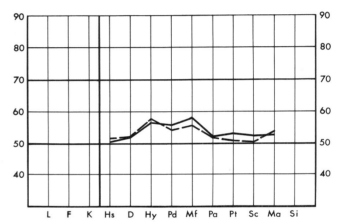

Figure 89a. Effect of Age (Male). *Solid Line*: Age Group 20–29 (N=46). *Broken Line*: Age Group 30–39 (N=45).

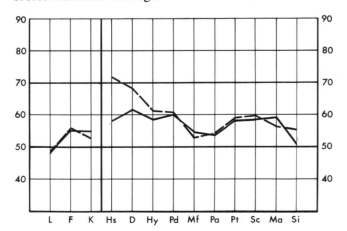

Figure 88. Effect of Age (Male). *Solid Line*: Age Group 20–29 (N=44). *Broken Line*: Age Group 50–59 (N=30).

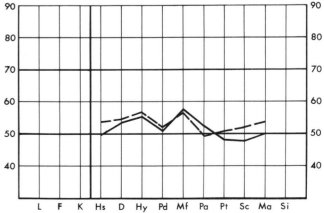

Figure 89b. Effect of Age (Male). *Solid Line*: Age Group 40–49 (N=21). *Broken Line*: Age Group 50–69 (N=25).

Study 89: EFFECT OF AGE (Canter, Day, Imboden, and Cluff, 1962). *See Figures 89a–89b.*

The subjects were randomly selected from civilians employed in an army chemical warfare center in Maryland. They were administered a slightly shortened form of the MMPI which included all the items necessary to score the validity scales and the standard nine clinical scales (the Si scale was excluded). Records having T-score values above 70 on the L and F scales were excluded from the study.

An analysis of variance among the four age groups showed no differences on any of the scales.

Study 90: OLD AGE (Swenson, 1961). *See Figure 90.*

The subjects were drawn from three separate sources: (a) so-called Golden Age Clubs; (b) homes for the aged; and (c) places of employment. There were 31 men and 64 women. The examiner met with the subjects individually or in small groups at their clubs or homes or

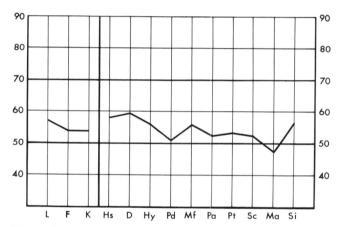

Figure 90. Old Age Group (Male and Female, N=95, Median Age 71, Age Range 60 Onward).

elsewhere, and described the project as a "study of interests and attitudes of the aged." The group form of the MMPI was used. An additional 115 subjects either refused to take the test, stopped before completing it, or obtained cannot say scores greater than 110. The median age of the 115 subjects who were not included in the sample was 75.

A distinct sex difference in the group occurred in the frequency of appearance of the Si scale as the high point in the profile, its presence being much more common among females.

Study 91: CEREBRAL PALSY (Linde and Patterson, 1958). *See Figure 91.*

The subjects were 14 males and 19 females with cerebral palsy. Twenty had a speech defect; 9 were confined to wheelchairs all the time and 3 part of the time, 3 used

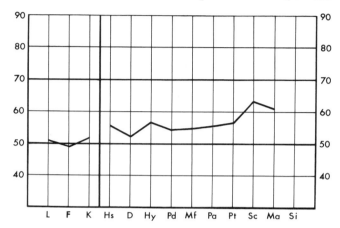

Figure 91. Cerebral Palsy Group (Male and Female, N=33, Mean Age 24, Age Range 20–43, Mean Education 11.4).

crutches, and the remainder were ambulatory. Only 3 had full use of both hands, the remainder having some use. Their socioeconomic backgrounds covered a wide range from unskilled labor to engineer, with a concentration in the middle occupational levels.

Study 92: CEREBRAL PALSY (Muthard, 1965). *See Figures 92a–92b.*

The cerebral palsy group was a stratified random sample of college students from a roster developed by corresponding with all likely sources of information about college students with cerebral palsy in the Midwest and the New York, Philadelphia, and Washington, D.C., areas. Stratification was done by age, sex, type of college, region, and severity (self-rating) variables. In their self-evaluation, 38 per cent of the group rated themselves as mildly impaired, 43 per cent as moderately severely impaired, and 18 per cent as severely impaired. For the 67 students for whom physicians' ratings were available, the following ratings were obtained: mild, 31 per cent; moderate, 37 per cent; severe, 31 per cent. On the basis of a modified index of social position taken from the method of Hollingshead and Redlich (1958), about one third of the group came from Class I and II families, another third from Class III, while the remaining third were from

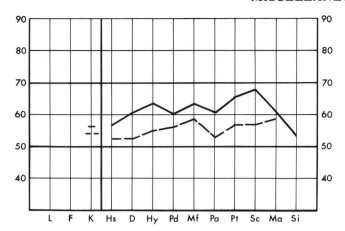

Figure 92a. Cerebral Palsy (Male). *Solid Line*: Cerebral Palsy Group (N=48, Median Age approx. 22). *Broken Line*: Normal Group (N=5035).

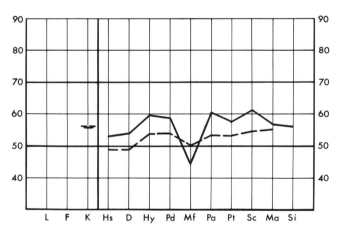

Figure 92b. Cerebral Palsy (Female). *Solid Line*: Cerebral Palsy Group (N=28, Median Age approx. 22). *Broken Line*: Normal Group (N=5014).

Class IV and V families. In a majority of instances (58 per cent) the father's occupation was in the managerial and professional category. Seventeen per cent of the fathers were skilled workers, 12 per cent were farmers, and the remainder were classified as clerical, sales, semiskilled, or unskilled workers. The booklet form of the MMPI was used. The normal control samples were taken from Goodstein's (1954) study of college males and from Black's (1956) study of college females.

The male cerebral palsy group scored higher than the male normal group on all the clinical scales except Ma. The female cerebral palsy group scored higher than the female normals on the D, Hy, Pd, Pa, Pt, and Si scales and lower on the Mf scale.

Study 93: DEAF COLLEGE STUDENTS (Rosen, 1966). *See Figure 93.*

The subjects were the majority of the 1963 entering class at Gallaudet College for the Deaf in Washington, D.C. Testing was done mainly in groups, although a few students were individually tested. The testing method was unusual, since proctors were provided to answer questions and to define as simply as possible words and idioms that students could not understand. While this was a violation of the usual procedure of administration, it was felt that it would reduce students' frustration and also provide information about the kinds of difficulty they were having. Eighty-six per cent of the students perceived themselves to be deaf or severely impaired auditorily. The stated age of onset of the hearing impediment was below three years for 85 per cent of the total group and below five years for 94 per cent.

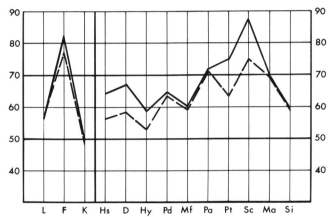

Figure 93. Deaf College Students. *Solid Line*: Males (N=96, Median Age 20). *Broken Line*: Females (N=83, Median Age 19).

The deaf males were compared with Goodstein's (1954) male college norms, and the deaf females were compared with Black's (1956) female college norms. For males, deaf students were higher on all scales. For females, deaf students were higher on all scales except Hy. Almost all differences were beyond the .001 level of significance. Clinical impressions did not support acceptance of the test results as interpretable in the same way as for hearing persons, and it was concluded that the MMPI should, for the time being, be used only as a research instrument with the deaf.

Study 94: DRIVERS (Brown and Berdie, 1960). *See Figure 94.*

The subjects were drawn from an initial sample of 933 freshmen who had registered for the General Education program at the University of Minnesota. The groups were selected in conjunction with an examination of the Department of Highway's files.

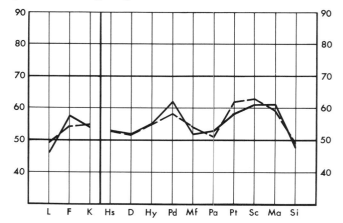

Figure 94. Drivers (Male). *Solid Line*: Poor Group (N=100, Mean Age approx. 19, Age Range 18–25). *Broken Line*: Good Group (N=100, Mean Age approx. 19, Age Range 18–25).

The poor group consisted of the 100 persons with the poorest driving records. These subjects had had five or more violations and/or three or more accidents. The good group had neither been convicted of a violation nor been involved in an accident. (A middle group was also included in the original study.)

The poor group scored higher than the good group on the Pd and Ma scales.

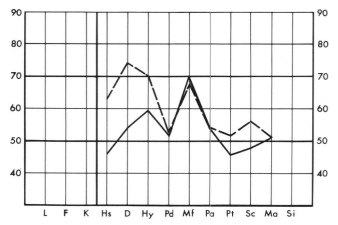

Figure 95a. Experimental Semistarvation (Male, N=32). *Solid Line*: Control Tests. *Broken Line*: Starvation Tests. Note: These profiles are not K-corrected.

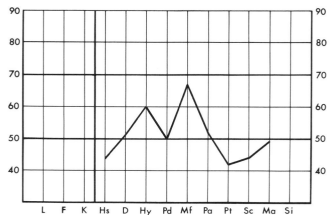

Figure 95b. Rehabilitation Group Tests in Semistarvation Experiment (Same Subjects as Figure 95a). Note: This profile is not K-corrected.

Study 95: EXPERIMENTAL SEMISTARVATION (Schiele and Brozek, 1948). *See Figures 95a–95b.*

The subjects were conscientious objectors during World War II who volunteered for a starvation-rehabilitation experiment at the University of Minnesota in 1944 and 1945. The primary purpose of the experiment was to investigate, under controlled conditions, the relative effectiveness of different types of diet in bringing about a recovery from prolonged inanition.

The control tests were given before the semistarvation period. The semistarvation tests were given at the end of the next 24 weeks, when the average daily intake was reduced to 1570 calories. The rehabilitation tests were given after 33 weeks of subsequent refeeding.

Study 96: HOMOSEXUALITY (Dean and Richardson, 1964). *See Figure 96.*

The homosexual group consisted of college-educated overt homosexuals. Two of the subjects had obtained doctor's degrees, 16 master's degrees, 19 bachelor's degrees, and 3 were still undergraduates. Their academic and occupational background was quite heterogeneous, with approximately 20 different academic majors and/or occupations represented. All were either employed or continuing their education and were thus functioning at least adequately in society. At the time of testing only two of the subjects were in some form of psychotherapy, and none were in legal difficulties for homosexual behavior. The heterosexual group consisted of graduate students who were within one year of obtaining their final degree

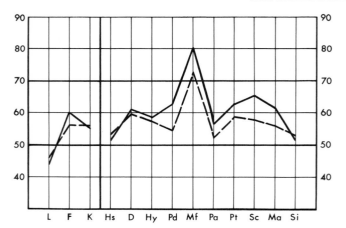

Figure 96. Homosexuality (Male). *Solid Line*: Homosexuals (N=40, Mean Age 29, Age Range 20–42). *Broken Line*: Heterosexuals (N=40, Mean Age 28, Age Range 22–35).

(in most cases the Ph.D.). They were the 40 of Barron's (1963) sample of 80 for whom MMPI data were available. The larger sample of 80 was academically heterogeneous, representing majors from 14 different academic departments.

The homosexual group scored higher than the heterosexual group on the Pd, Mf, Sc, and Ma scales.

Study 97: HEIGHT (Hood, 1963). *See Figure 97.*

The subjects were drawn from more than 10,000 freshmen who had entered the University of Minnesota over a nine-year period, and for whom MMPI scores and height data were available.

The tall group was drawn from the 3.1 per cent who were 75 inches or taller. The short group was drawn from the 3.7 per cent who were 65 inches or shorter.

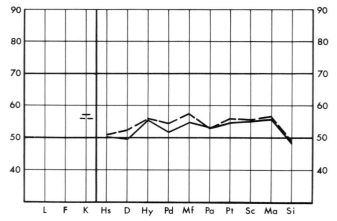

Figure 97. Height (Male). *Solid Line*: Tall Group (N=150). *Broken Line*: Short Group (N=150).

The short group scored higher than the tall group on the D and Mf scales.

Study 98: PASTORAL COUNSELING CLIENTS (Wagner and Dobbins, 1967). *See Figure 98.*

The subjects were Assembly of God parishioners. All were administered the MMPI by the minister. No subject had an L scale raw score of more than 10, or omitted more than 35–40 items.

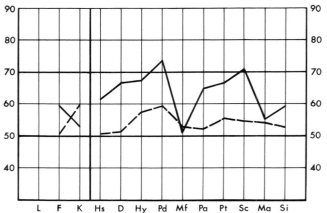

Figure 98. Pastoral Counseling Clients (Male and Female). *Solid Line*: Counseling Group (N=40, Mean Age 28, Mean Education 11.8). *Broken Line*: No Counseling Group (N=40, Mean Age 29, Mean Education 11.9).

The counseling group had sought aid in pastoral counseling over a consecutive ten-month period. All came to the minister of their own accord. There were 13 males and 27 females. The no counseling group was selected from among parishioners who had not sought counseling. An effort was made to choose a group which was demographically similar to the counseling group.

The counseling group scored higher than the no counseling group on the F, Hs, D, Hy, Pd, Pa, Pt, Sc, and Si scales and lower on the K scale.

Study 99: PREGNANCY (Hooke and Marks, 1962). *See Figure 99.*

The pregnant group consisted of women in the eighth month of their first pregnancy. They were Minnesota residents participating voluntarily in a longitudinal study of prenatal factors in child development at the University of Minnesota Hospitals. The nonpregnant group was the MMPI normative sample as reported by Hathaway and Briggs (1957).

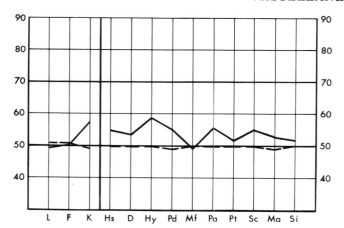

Figure 99. Pregnancy. *Solid Line*: Pregnant Group (N=24, Mean Age 23.7, Age Range 21–28). *Broken Line*: Nonpregnant Women (N=315).

The pregnant women scored higher than the nonpregnant group on the K, Hy, Pd, Pa, Sc, Ma, and Es scales. In addition, the high-point frequency of Pd in the pregnant group (21.8 per cent) was significantly greater than in the normative group (8.4 per cent). Testing for a percentage difference of abnormal (70+) scores between groups failed, however, to yield a reliable split.

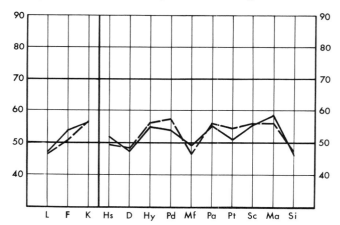

Figure 100. Susceptibility to Hypnosis (Female). *Solid Line*: Highly Susceptible Group (N=16). *Broken Line*: Unsusceptible Group (N=19).

Study 100: SUSCEPTIBILITY TO HYPNOSIS (Schulman and London, 1963). *See Figure 100.*

The subjects were drawn from 87 female undergraduates who had volunteered to participate in a hypnosis experiment, and who had been administered the Stanford Hypnotic Suggestibility Scale, Form A. Subjects were classified into four groups of relative hypnotic susceptibility. The questionnaire form of the MMPI was used. Subjects were not informed of their precise susceptibility ratings.

The highly susceptible group consisted of those who scored 10–12 on the SHSA. The unsusceptible group consisted of those who scored 0–4 on the SHSA.

Statistical analyses (which included two additional groups) indicated that the highly susceptible group scored lower on the Pd and Pt scales than the other groups.

Study 101: STUTTERING (Lanyon, 1966). *See Figure 101.*

The subjects were drawn from more than 200 stutterers attending the University of Iowa Speech Clinic between 1956 and 1962, and included all who met the following criteria: (a) college age or older; (b) first appear-

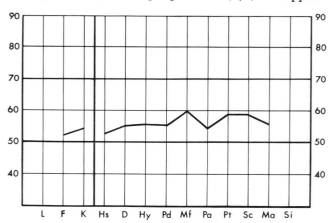

Figure 101. Stutterers (Male and Female, N=25, Mean Age 22, Age Range 17–32, Mean IQ 116, IQ Range 96–142).

ance at the clinic; (c) therapist's rating of "average" or greater in stuttering severity; (d) valid (L below 7, K below 23, F below 16) MMPI completed within a month of beginning therapy. The sample represented approximately the severest one third of the clinic's stuttering population. Most of the subjects were college students or graduates.

63

Study 102: BOOKLET AND CARD ADMINISTRA-
TION (Rosen, Hales, and Peek, 1958). *See Figure
102.*

The subjects were patients admitted to the psychiatry
section of the Minneapolis VA Hospital.

The booklet form of the MMPI was administered to
every other patient admitted (with the exception of a few
confused patients), until a sample of 75 was obtained.
Forty-eight per cent of those who had taken the booklet
form were diagnosed as neurotic, 23 per cent as psy-

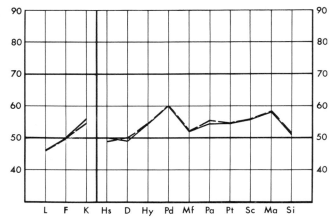

Figure 103a. Booklet and Oral Administration for Nurses
(Female, N=58). *Solid Line*: Booklet Tests. *Broken Line*:
Oral Tests.

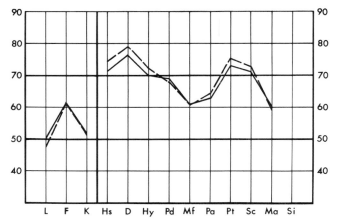

Figure 102. Booklet and Card Administration (Male). *Solid
Line*: Booklet Tests (N=75). *Broken Line*: Card Tests (N=
250).

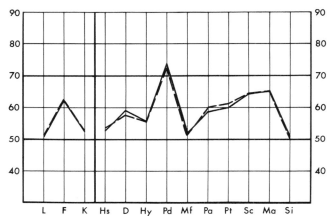

Figure 103b. Booklet and Oral Administration for Literate
Prisoners (Male, N=120). *Solid Line*: Booklet Tests. *Broken
Line*: Oral Tests.

chotic, and 20 per cent as having a personality disorder;
9 per cent had other diagnoses. The card form of the
MMPI was taken by a comparison group of patients. This
sample was representative of all new, white, male, testable veterans in the hospital over a two-year period.
Fifty-six per cent of those who had taken the card form
were diagnosed as neurotic, 23 per cent as psychotic, and
12 per cent as having a personality disorder; 9 per cent
had other diagnoses.

No differences were found between the samples on any
of the regular scales.

Study 103: BOOKLET AND ORAL ADMINISTRA-
TION (Wolf, Freinek, and Shaffer, 1964). *See Figures
103a–103c.*

The booklet and oral forms of the MMPI were both
administered to three different subject groups. In each

case, half the subjects in each group were given the oral
form first followed by the booklet form one day later; for
the remainder of each group, this procedure was reversed.
The oral presentation was given in groups of about 30,
using a single tape-recorder. All the MMPI items were
used; they had been recorded under studio conditions
by a professional announcer. A conversational tone
was used for the items, which were spaced six seconds
apart.

The first group consisted of student nurses in a state
mental hospital. The second group consisted of literate
penitentiary inmates, scoring at a sixth-grade reading

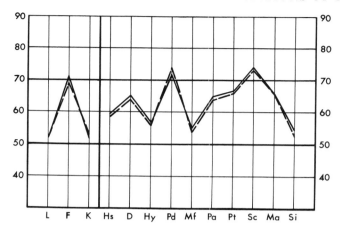

Figure 103c. Booklet and Oral Administration for Semiliterate Prisoners (Male, N=120). *Solid Line*: Booklet Tests. *Broken Line*: Oral Tests.

level and above, and selected consecutively from youthful offenders admitted over a six-month period. The third group consisted of semiliterate penitentiary inmates, scoring below a sixth-grade reading level but still able to complete the booklet form of the MMPI, and otherwise meeting the same criteria as the second group. (The penitentiary groups are compared in Study 64.)

There were no differences between forms for any group on any of the regular MMPI scales. A comparison of first and second test presentations investigated the effects on mean scores of retesting within a short period. Scores on the first presentation were higher on the Hs, D, Hy, Pt, and Si scales in each of the three groups and lower on the K scale.

Study 104: BOOKLET AND ORAL ADMINISTRATION (Urmer, Black, and Wendland, 1960). *See Figure 104.*

The booklet and oral (taped) forms of the MMPI were administered to 39 male and 2 female patients who were residing in the Rancho Los Amigos Hospital, Downey, California, for placement rather than medical problems. The order of presentation was randomly determined, with 22 patients taking the booklet form first and 19 taking the tape form first, and with time intervals between administrations ranging from one week to three months. In the taped form, items 1–375, 383, 398, 406, 461, and 502 were recorded. Each item was preceded by its number and followed by a five-second interval to permit the recording of the response on the standard IBM answer sheet. Each patient had an individual speaker or earphone, and was given an opportunity at the completion of the test to answer any skipped item.

There were no significant differences between the means on any of the scales.

Study 105: EFFECT OF STRESS (Eschenbach and Dupree, 1959). *See Figure 105.*

The subjects were United States Air Force officers and airmen who were victims of extreme environmental changes in an unfamiliar situation. They acted as subjects during field tests which were primarily designed to test air force liferaft survival equipment in a survival stress situation. There were 10 volunteers and 12 non-volunteers; these groups underwent different experiences.

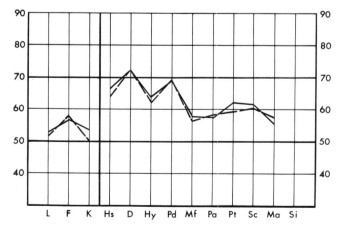

Figure 104. Booklet and Oral Administration (Male and Female, N=41). *Solid Line*: Booklet Tests. *Broken Line*: Oral Tests.

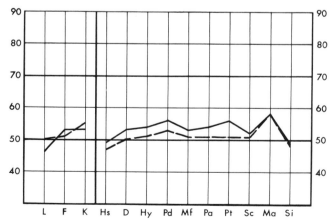

Figure 105. Effect of Stress (Male, N=22, Mean Age 29, Age Range 20–40). *Solid Line*: Pre-Stress Tests. *Broken Line*: Post-Stress Tests.

The pre-stress MMPI was administered on the day before the survival experience, when the prevailing atmosphere was one of good humor. The post-stress test was administered directly after the experience, and the testing atmosphere was drastically changed. The members of the group undergoing the first survival test (the volunteers) were physically sick and fatigued from the liferaft ordeal, and feebly protested having to retake the MMPI. The group undergoing the second survival test (the nonvolunteers) at first strongly protested the retest, then lapsed into grim silence and sought to stay awake to complete the MMPI. The situation was described by the participant-observer as one of stress, seriousness, and fatigue.

The post-stress scores were higher than the pre-stress scores on the L scale and lower on the Hs, Pd, Pt, Sc, and A scales.

Study 106: FAKE GOOD FALSIFICATION BY NORMALS (Exner, McDowell, Pabst, Stackman, and Kirk, 1963). *See Figure 106.*

College students (13 males and 12 females) were asked to respond to the MMPI in such a manner as to appear "normal" or socially desirable, as would an attractive applicant for job or school. These were the "fake good" scores. In a second administration, the same students were asked to respond to the MMPI again, but this time in a completely honest manner as if they were interested in gaining information concerning themselves. For this administration, their names were not written on the answer sheets.

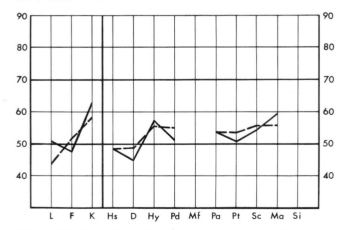

Figure 106. Fake Good Falsification by Normals (Male and Female, N=25). *Solid Line:* Fake Good Tests. *Broken Line:* Honest Tests.

The honest profiles were higher than the fake good profiles on the F and Pd scales and the F minus K and L plus K scale combinations and lower on the L and K scales.

Study 107: FAKE BAD FALSIFICATION BY NORMALS (Exner, McDowell, Pabst, Stackman, and Kirk, 1963). *See Figure 107.*

College students (12 males and 13 females) were asked to respond to the MMPI in a manner sufficiently deviant so that they would be exempt from some social responsibility such as military service but not so deviant that institutionalization would be required. These were the "fake bad" scores. In a second administration, the same students were asked to respond in a completely honest manner as if they were interested in gaining information concerning themselves. For this administration, their names were not written on the answer sheets.

The fake bad profiles were higher than the honest profiles on all the clinical scales, on the F scale, and on the F minus K scale combination. They were lower on the K scale.

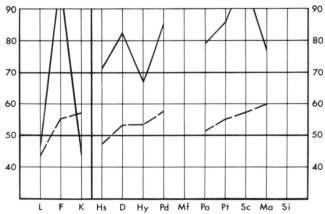

Figure 107. Fake Bad Falsification by Normals (Male and Female, N=25). *Solid Line:* Fake Bad Tests. *Broken Line:* Honest Tests.

Study 108: RETEST STABILITY (Hathaway and Monachesi, 1963). *See Figures 108a–108b.*

The subjects were drawn from twelve schools which were representative of the state of Minnesota as far as possible with respect to economic and geographic areas. They were tested in the ninth grade and again in the twelfth grade. Thus the test-retest interval was approximately three years. All subjects included gave valid pro-

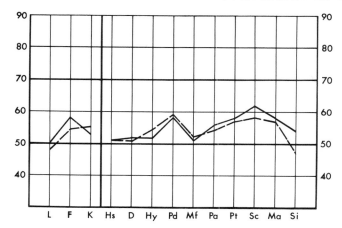

Figure 108a. Retest Stability (Male, N=1922). *Solid Line*: Original Tests (Mean Age 15.1). *Broken Line*: Retests (Mean Age approx. 18.1).

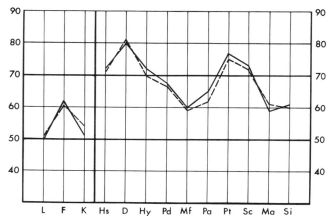

Figure 109. Retest Stability (Male, N=40, Median Age 32, Median Education 11.2). *Solid Line*: Original Tests. *Broken Line*: Retests.

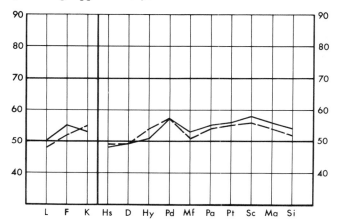

Figure 108b. Retest Stability (Female, N=2054). *Solid Line*: Original Tests (Mean Age 14.8). *Broken Line*: Retests (Mean Age approx. 17.8).

files (L less than 10, F less than 16) on both the original test and the retest.

For the boys the retest was higher than the original test on the K, Hy, Pd, and Mf scales and lower on the L, F, D, Pa, Pt, Sc, Ma, and Si scales. For the girls the retest was higher than the original test on the K, Hs, and Hy scales and lower on the L, F, Mf, Pa, Pt, Sc, Ma, and Si scales.

Study 109: RETEST STABILITY (Rosen, 1953). *See Figure 109.*

The subjects were male patients admitted for the first time to the psychiatric section of the Minneapolis VA Hospital during an eight-week period. Retesting was done within two to seven days until 40 test-retest cases

were obtained. All patients took the individual form of the MMPI. None were in active service. The first test was given 0–12 days after admission, but usually within 3 days. Thirteen of the subjects had never been married. Twenty-two had an IQ equivalent of 110 or higher. There were 25 with a primary diagnosis of neurosis (mainly anxiety reaction or depressive reaction), and 11 were diagnosed psychotic.

The retest was higher than the original test on the K scale, and lower on the Pa scale (and on the K-uncorrected Pd, Pt, and Sc scales). Test-retest correlations ranged from .55 to .88.

Study 110: RETEST STABILITY (Warman and Hannum, 1965). *See Figure 110.*

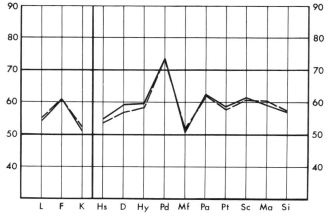

Figure 110. Retest Stability (Female, N=50, Median Age 24, Age Range 14–50). *Solid Line*: Admission Tests. *Broken Line*: Retests.

The subjects were consecutively admitted prisoners at the Iowa Women's Reformatory. Median sentence, educational level, marital status, and variety of offenses were typical of the characteristics of incarcerated women. The admission test was administered within three weeks of arrival at the institution, as part of the routine intake processing. The retest was administered six months later.

There were no differences between the profiles on any of the regular scales.

Study 111: SIMULATION OF "IDEAL SELF" (Rapaport, 1958). *See Figure 111.*

The subjects were military personnel who were psychiatric patients. They were drawn over a six-month period from the psychiatric facilities of an army basic training center. Thirty-three were seen as outpatient referrals, and 15 were psychiatric inpatients. Twelve were diagnosed schizophrenia, 11 "no neuropsychiatric disease," 20 character and behavior problems, 2 psychotic depression, and 3 epilepsy. The real self profiles were gathered under regular conditions of administration. The ideal self profiles were gathered immediately thereafter under an "ideal self" instructional set.

The real self profiles were higher than the ideal self

profiles on all validity and clinical scales except Ma. An examination of follow-up data for the patients with a positive psychiatric diagnosis showed no significant relationship between prognosis and ability to improve one's MMPI performance under ideal self instructions.

Study 112: SIMULATION OF "NORMALCY" (Grayson and Olinger, 1957). *See Figure 112.*

The regular profiles were gathered through routine administration of the MMPI to 45 consecutively hospitalized males as they entered a psychiatric hospital. Twenty-four were diagnosed schizophrenia, 13 character disorder, 4 manic depressive, and 4 psychoneurosis. The simulated normal profiles were gathered on the day following the regular administration. The patients were instructed to answer "the way a typical, well-adjusted person on the outside would do."

The regular profiles were higher than the simulated normal profiles on the F, Hs, D, Hy, Pd, Pa, Pt, and Sc scales and lower on the K scale and the K minus F scale combination. Examination of each patient's hospital status after three months showed a significant relationship between prognosis and MMPI performance under simulated normal instructions.

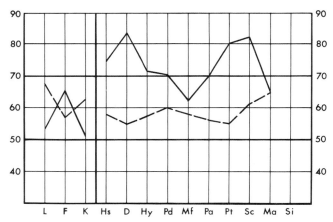

Figure 111. Simulation of "Ideal Self" (Male, N=48). *Solid Line*: Real Self Tests. *Broken Line*: Ideal Self Tests.

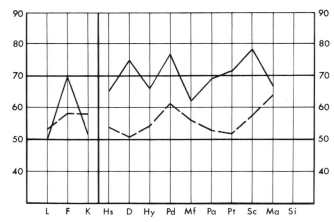

Figure 112. Simulation of "Normalcy" (Male, N=45). *Solid Line*: Regular Tests. *Broken Line*: Simulated Normal Tests.

REFERENCES

References

American Psychiatric Association. *Diagnostic and statistical manual: mental disorders.* Washington: American Psychiatric Association Mental Hospital Service, 1952.

Andersen, A. L., and L. J. Hanvik. The psychometric localization of brain lesions: the differential effect of frontal and parietal lesions on MMPI profiles. *Journal of Clinical Psychology*, 1950, 6, 177–180.

Apfeldorf, M., J. L. Scheinker, and G. L. Whitman. MMPI responses of aged domiciled veterans with disciplinary records. *Journal of Consulting Psychology*, 1966, 30, 362.

Ashbaugh, J. H. Personality patterns of juvenile delinquents in an area of small population. In S. R. Hathaway and E. D. Monachesi (Eds.), *Analyzing and predicting juvenile delinquency with the MMPI.* Minneapolis: University of Minnesota Press, 1953.

Baer, D. J., and J. F. Moynihan. Stepwise discriminant-function analysis of seminary-candidate MMPI scores. *Journal of Psychology*, 1964, 58, 413–419.

Ball, J. C. Comparison of MMPI profile differences among Negro-white adolescents. *Journal of Clinical Psychology*, 1960, 16, 304–307.

——. *Social deviancy and adolescent personality.* Lexington: University of Kentucky Press, 1962.

Barron, F. An ego-strength scale which predicts response to psychotherapy. *Journal of Consulting Psychology*, 1953, 17, 327–333. (a)

——. Some test correlates of response to psychotherapy. *Journal of Consulting Psychology*, 1953, 17, 235–241. (b)

Bier, W. C., S.J. Comparative study of a seminary group and four other groups on the Minnesota Multiphasic Personality Inventory. *Studies in Psychology and Psychiatry from the Catholic University of America*, 1948, 7, 1–107.

Black, J. D. The interpretation of MMPI profiles of college women. Doctoral dissertation, University of Minnesota, 1953. Reprinted in part in G. S. Welsh and W. G. Dahlstrom (Eds.), *Basic readings on the MMPI in psychology and medicine.* Minneapolis: University of Minnesota Press, 1956.

Brown, P. L., and R. F. Berdie. Driver behavior and scores on the MMPI. *Journal of Applied Psychology*, 1960, 44, 18–21.

Butcher, J., B. Ball, and E. Ray. Effects of socio-economic level on MMPI differences in Negro-white college students. *Journal of Counseling Psychology*, 1964, 11, 83–87.

Cabeen, C. W., and J. C. Coleman. Group therapy with sex offenders: description and evaluation of a group therapy program in an institutional setting. *Journal of Clinical Psychology*, 1961, 17, 122–129.

Calden, G., and J. E. Hokanson. The influence of age on MMPI responses. *Journal of Clinical Psychology*, 1959, 15, 194–195.

Canter, A. H. MMPI profiles in multiple sclerosis. *Journal of Consulting Psychology*, 1951, 15, 253–256.

Canter, A., C. W. Day, J. B. Imboden, and L. E. Cluff. The influence of age and health status on the MMPI scores of a normal population. *Journal of Clinical Psychology*, 1962, 18, 71–73.

Capwell, D. F. Personality patterns of adolescent girls: delinquents and non-delinquents. *Journal of Applied Psychology*, 1945, 29, 289–297. Reprinted in part in S. R. Hathaway and E. D. Monachesi (Eds.), *Analyzing and predicting juvenile delinquency with the MMPI.* Minneapolis: University of Minnesota Press, 1953.

Clark, J. H. The relationship between MMPI scores and psychiatric classification of army general prisoners. *Journal of Clinical Psychology*, 1952, 8, 86–89.

Comrey, A. L. A factor analysis of items on the MMPI depression scale. *Educational and Psychological Measurement*, 1957, 17, 578–585.

Dahlstrom, W. G., and G. S. Welsh. *An MMPI handbook.* Minneapolis: University of Minnesota Press, 1960.

Dean, R. B., and H. Richardson. Analysis of MMPI profiles of forty college-educated overt male homosexuals. *Journal of Consulting Psychology*, 1964, 28, 483–486.

Doehring, D. G., and R. M. Reitan. MMPI performance of aphasic and nonaphasic brain-damaged patients. *Journal of Clinical Psychology*, 1960, 16, 307–309.

Drake, L. E. A social I.E. scale for the MMPI. *Journal of Applied Psychology*, 1946, 30, 51–54.

—— and E. R. Oetting. *An MMPI codebook for counselors.* Minneapolis: University of Minnesota Press, 1959.

Dragsow, J., and J. McKenzie. College transcripts, graduation, and the MMPI. *Journal of Counseling Psychology*, 1958, 5, 196–199.

Eichman, W. J. Discrimination of female schizophrenics with configural analysis of the MMPI profile. *Journal of Consulting Psychology*, 1959, 23, 442–447.

Eschenbach, A. E., and L. Dupree. The influence of stress on MMPI scale scores. *Journal of Clinical Psychology*, 1959, 15, 42–45.

Exner, J. E., E. McDowell, J. Pabst, W. Stackman, and L. Kirk. On the detection of willful falsifications in the MMPI. *Journal of Consulting Psychology*, 1963, 27, 91–94.

Farberow, N. L. Personality patterns of suicidal mental patients. *Genetic Psychology Monographs*, 1950, 42, 3–80.

Feldman, M. J. The use of the MMPI profile for prognosis and evaluation of shock therapy. *Journal of Consulting Psychology*, 1952, 16, 376–382.

Fricke, B. G. Conversion hysterics and the MMPI. *Journal of Clinical Psychology*, 1956, 12, 322–326.

Gilberstadt, H., and J. Duker. *A Handbook for clinical and actuarial MMPI interpretation*. Philadelphia: Saunders, 1965.

Gilberstadt, H., and E. Farkas. Another look at MMPI profile types in multiple sclerosis. *Journal of Consulting Psychology*, 1961, 25, 440–444.

Good, P. K., and J. P. Brantner. *The physician's guide to the MMPI*. Minneapolis: University of Minnesota Press, 1961.

Goodstein, L. D. Regional differences in MMPI responses among male college students. *Journal of Consulting Psychology*, 1954, 18, 437–441.

———— and V. N. Rowley. A further study of MMPI differences between parents of disturbed and nondisturbed children. *Journal of Consulting Psychology*, 1961, 25, 460.

Gough, H. G. The F minus K dissimulation index for the Minnesota Multiphasic Personality Inventory. *Journal of Consulting Psychology*, 1950, 14, 408–413.

Grayson, H. M., and L. B. Olinger. Simulation of "normalcy" by psychiatric patients on the MMPI. *Journal of Consulting Psychology*, 1957, 21, 73–77.

Guthrie, G. M. Six MMPI diagnostic profile patterns. *Journal of Psychology*, 1950, 30, 317–323.

Hanvik, L. J. MMPI profiles in patients with low back pain. *Journal of Consulting Psychology*, 1951, 15, 350–353.

———— and M. Byrum. MMPI profiles of parents of child psychiatric patients. *Journal of Clinical Psychology*, 1959, 15, 427–431.

Harris, R. E., and J. C. Lingoes. Subscales for the MMPI: an aid to profile interpretation. Mimeographed. San Francisco: Department of Psychiatry, University of California, 1955.

Hathaway, S. R. Scales 5 (Masculinity-femininity), 6 (Paranoia), and 8 (Schizophrenia). In G. S. Welsh and W. G. Dahlstrom (Eds.), *Basic readings on the MMPI in psychology and medicine*. Minneapolis: University of Minnesota Press, 1956.

————. Foreword. In W. G. Dahlstrom and G. S. Welsh, *An MMPI handbook*. Minneapolis: University of Minnesota Press, 1960.

———— and P. F. Briggs. Some normative data on new MMPI scales. *Journal of Clinical Psychology*, 1957, 13, 364–368.

Hathaway, S. R., and J. C. McKinley. A multiphasic personality schedule (Minnesota): I. Construction of the Schedule. *Journal of Psychology*, 1940, 10, 249–254.

————. A multiphasic personality schedule (Minnesota): III. The measurement of symptomatic depression. *Journal of Psychology*, 1942, 14, 73–84.

————. *The Minnesota Multiphasic Personality Inventory manual*. Revised. New York: The Psychological Corporation, 1951.

Hathaway, S. R., and P. E. Meehl. *An atlas for the clinical use of the MMPI*. Minneapolis: University of Minnesota Press, 1951.

Hathaway, S. R., and E. D. Monachesi. Personality characteristics of adolescents as related to their later careers. In S. R. Hathaway and E. D. Monachesi (Eds.), *Analyzing and predicting juvenile delinquency with the MMPI*. Minneapolis: University of Minnesota Press, 1953.

————. *Adolescent personality and behavior*. Minneapolis: University of Minnesota Press, 1963.

Heilbrun, A. B. Revision of the MMPI K correction procedure for improved detection of maladjustment in a normal college population. *Journal of Consulting Psychology*, 1963, 27, 161–165.

Hill, H. E., C. A. Haertzen, and R. Glaser. Personality characteristics of narcotic addicts as indicated by the MMPI. *Journal of General Psychology*, 1960, 62, 127–139.

Hokanson, J. E., and G. Calden. Negro-white differences on the MMPI. *Journal of Clinical Psychology*, 1960, 16, 32–33.

Hollingshead, A. B., and F. C. Redlich. *Social class and mental illness*. New York: Wiley, 1958.

Hood, A. B. A study of the relationship between physique and personality variables as measured by the MMPI. *Journal of Personality*, 1963, 31, 97–107.

Hooke, J. F., and P. A. Marks. MMPI characteristics of pregnancy. *Journal of Clinical Psychology*, 1962, 18, 316–317.

Hovey, H. B. Somatization and other neurotic reactions and MMPI profiles. *Journal of Clinical Psychology*, 1949, 5, 153–156.

Hoyt, D. P., and G. M. Sedlacek. Differentiating alcoholics from normals and abnormals with the MMPI. *Journal of Clinical Psychology*, 1958, 14, 69–74.

Jurjevich, R. M. Normative data for the clinical and additional MMPI scales for a population of delinquent girls. *Journal of General Psychology*, 1963, 69, 143–146.

Kennedy, W. A. MMPI profiles of gifted adolescents. *Journal of Clinical Psychology*, 1962, 18, 148–149.

Kingsley, L. MMPI profiles of psychopaths and prisoners. *Journal of Clinical Psychology*, 1960, 16, 302–304.

Klove, H., and D. G. Doehring. MMPI in epileptic groups with differential etiology. *Journal of Clinical Psychology*, 1962, 18, 149–153.

Lanyon, R. I. The MMPI and prognosis in stuttering therapy. *Journal of Speech and Hearing Disorders*, 1966, 31, 186–191.

Lauber, M., and W. G. Dahlstrom. MMPI findings in the rehabilitation of delinquent girls. In S. R. Hathaway and E. D. Monachesi (Eds.), *Analyzing and predicting juvenile delinquency with the MMPI*. Minneapolis: University of Minnesota Press, 1953.

Lauterbach, C. G., W. Vogel, and J. Hart. Comparison of the MMPIs of male problem adolescents and their parents. *Journal of Clinical Psychology*, 1962, 18, 485–487.

Levitt, H., and C. Fellner. MMPI profiles of three obesity subgroups. *Journal of Consulting Psychology*, 1965, 29, 91.

Linde, T., and C. H. Patterson. The MMPI in cerebral palsy. *Journal of Consulting Psychology*, 1958, 22, 210–212.

Liverant, S. MMPI differences between parents of disturbed and nondisturbed children. *Journal of Consulting Psychology*, 1959, 23, 256–260.

Lucero, R. J., and W. C. Currens. Effects of clinical training on personality functioning of the minister. *Journal of Clinical Psychology*, 1964, 20, 147.

McDonald, R. L., and M. D. Gynther. MMPI differences

associated with sex, race, and class in two adolescent samples. *Journal of Consulting Psychology*, 1963, 27, 112–116.

McKinley, J. C., and S. R. Hathaway. A multiphasic personality schedule (Minnesota): II. A differential study of hypochondriasis. *Journal of Psychology*, 1940, 10, 255–268.

———. A multiphasic personality schedule: IV: Psychasthenia. *Journal of Applied Psychology*, 1942, 26, 614–624.

———. The MMPI: V. Hysteria, hypomania, and psychopathic deviate. *Journal of Applied Psychology*, 1944, 28, 153–174.

McKinley, J. C., S. R. Hathaway, and P. E. Meehl. The MMPI: VI. The K scale. *Journal of Consulting Psychology*, 1948, 12, 20–31.

Marks, P. A. An assessment of the diagnostic process in a child guidance setting. *Psychological Monographs*, 1961, 75, No. 3 (Whole No. 507).

——— and W. Seeman. *The actuarial description of abnormal personality.* Baltimore: Williams and Wilkins, 1963.

Marsh, J. T., J. Hilliard, and R. Liechti. A sexual deviation scale for the MMPI. *Journal of Consulting Psychology*, 1955, 19, 55–59.

Meehl, P. E., and S. R. Hathaway. The K factor as a suppressor variable in the MMPI. *Journal of Applied Psychology*, 1946, 30, 525–564.

Meehl, P. E., and A. Rosen. Antecedent probability and the efficiency of psychometric signs, patterns, or cutting scores. *Psychological Bulletin*, 1955, 52, 194–216.

Miller, C., C. Wertz, and S. Counts. Racial differences on the MMPI. *Journal of Clinical Psychology*, 1961, 17, 159–161.

Miller, W. G., and T. E. Hannum. Characteristics of homosexually involved incarcerated females. *Journal of Consulting Psychology*, 1963, 27, 277.

Monachesi, E. D. The personality patterns of juvenile delinquents as indicated by the MMPI. In S. R. Hathaway and E. D. Monachesi (Eds.), *Analyzing and predicting juvenile delinquency with the MMPI.* Minneapolis: University of Minnesota Press, 1953.

Motto, J. J. The MMPI performance of veterans with organic and psychiatric disabilities. *Journal of Consulting Psychology*, 1958, 22, 304.

Muthard, J. E. MMPI findings for cerebral palsied college students. *Journal of Consulting Psychology*, 1965, 29, 599.

Muzekari, L. H. The MMPI in predicting treatment outcome in alcoholism. *Journal of Consulting Psychology*, 1965, 29, 281.

Norman, R. D., and M. Redlo. MMPI personality patterns for various college major groups. *Journal of Applied Psychology*, 1952, 36, 404–409.

Olson, R. W. MMPI sex differences in narcotic addicts. *Journal of General Psychology*, 1964, 71, 257–266.

Panton, J. H. MMPI profile configurations among crime classification groups. *Journal of Clinical Psychology*, 1959, 15, 305–308.

———. The identification of habitual criminalism with the MMPI. *Journal of Clinical Psychology*, 1962, 18, 133–136. (a)

———. The identification of predispositional factors in self-mutilation within a state prison population. *Journal of Clinical Psychology*, 1962, 18, 63–67. (b)

Peterson, D. R. The diagnosis of subclinical schizophrenia. *Journal of Consulting Psychology*, 1954, 18, 198-200. (a)

———. Predicting hospitalization of psychiatric outpatients. *Journal of Abnormal and Social Psychology*, 1954, 49, 260–265. (b)

Randolph, M. H., H. Richardson, and R. C. Johnson. A comparison of social and solitary male delinquents. *Journal of Consulting Psychology*, 1961, 25, 293–295.

Rapaport, G. M. "Ideal self" instructions, MMPI profile changes, and the prediction of clinical improvement. *Journal of Consulting Psychology*, 1958, 22, 459–463.

Rempel, P. P. The use of multivariate statistical analysis of Minnesota Multiphasic Personality Inventory scores in the classification of delinquent and nondelinquent high school boys. *Journal of Consulting Psychology*, 1958, 22, 17–23.

Rosen, A. Test-retest stability of MMPI scales for a psychiatric population. *Journal of Consulting Psychology*, 1953, 17, 217–221.

———. Differentiation of diagnostic groups by individual MMPI scales. *Journal of Consulting Psychology*, 1958, 22, 453–457.

———. MMPI responses of deaf college preparatory students. Paper presented at the annual meeting of the American Psychological Association, New York, September 1966.

———, W. M. Hales, and R. M. Peek. Comparability of MMPI card and booklet forms for psychiatric patients. *Journal of Clinical Psychology*, 1958, 14, 387–388.

Rosen, A. C. A comparative study of alcoholic and psychiatric patients with the MMPI. *Quarterly Journal of Studies on Alcohol*, 1960, 21, 253–266.

Rosen, E., and G. B. Rizzo. Preliminary standardization of the MMPI for use in Italy: a case study in intercultural and intracultural differences. *Educational and Psychological Measurement*, 1961, 21, 629–636.

Rowley, V. N., and F. B. Stone. MMPI differences between emotionally disturbed and delinquent adolescents. *Journal of Clinical Psychology*, 1962, 18, 481–484.

Schiele, B. C., and J. Brozek. "Experimental neurosis" resulting from semistarvation in man. *Psychosomatic Medicine*, 1948, 10, 31–50.

Schneider, L., and S. Lysgaard. The deferred gratification pattern. *American Sociological Review*, 1953, 18, 142–149.

Schofield, W. Changes in responses to the Minnesota Multiphasic Inventory following certain therapies. *Psychological Monographs*, 1950, 64, No. 5 (Whole No. 311).

———. A study of medical students with the MMPI: II. Group and individual changes after two years. *Journal of Psychology*, 1953, 36, 137–141.

———. Changes following certain therapies as reflected in the MMPI. In G. S. Welsh and W. G. Dahlstrom (Eds.), *Basic readings on the MMPI in psychology and medicine.* Minneapolis: University of Minnesota Press, 1956.

Schulman, R. E., and P. London. Hypnotic susceptibility

and MMPI profiles. *Journal of Consulting Psychology*, 1963, 27, 157–160.

Shaffer, J. W., K. Y. Ota, and T. E. Hanlon. The comparative validity of several MMPI indices of severity of psychopathology. *Journal of Clinical Psychology*, 1964, 20, 467–473.

Shontz, F. C. MMPI responses of patients with multiple sclerosis. *Journal of Consulting Psychology*, 1955, 19, 74.

Silver, R. J., and L. K. Sines. MMPI characteristics of a state hospital population. *Journal of Clinical Psychology*, 1961, 17, 142–146.

Spiaggia, M. An investigation of the personality traits of art students. *Educational and Psychological Measurement*, 1950, 10, 285–293.

Stone, F. B., and V. N. Rowley. MMPI differences between emotionally disturbed and delinquent adolescent girls. *Journal of Clinical Psychology*, 1963, 19, 227–230.

Stone, F. B., V. N. Rowley, and J. C. MacQueen. Using the MMPI with adolescents who have somatic symptoms. *Psychological Reports*, 1966, 18, 139–147.

Sullivan, P. L., C. Miller, and W. Smelser. Factors of length of stay and progress in psychotherapy. *Journal of Consulting Psychology*, 1958, 22, 1–9.

Sullivan, P. L., and G. S. Welsh. A technique for objective configurational analysis of MMPI profiles. *Journal of Consulting Psychology*, 1952, 16, 383–388.

Sulzer, E. S. The effects of promazine on MMPI performance in the chronic psychiatric patient. *Psychopharmacologia*, 1961, 2, 137–140.

Sundberg, N. D. The use of the MMPI for cross-cultural personality study: a preliminary report on the German translation. *Journal of Abnormal and Social Psychology*, 1956, 53, 281–283.

Swenson, W. M. Structured personality testing in the aged: an MMPI study of the gerontic population. *Journal of Clinical Psychology*, 1961, 17, 302–304.

——— and B. P. Grimes. Characteristics of sex offenders admitted to a Minnesota state hospital for pre-sentence psychiatric investigation. *Psychiatric Quarterly Supplement*, 1958, 31, 110–123.

Taft, R. A cross-cultural comparison of the MMPI. *Journal of Consulting Psychology*, 1957, 21, 161–164.

———. A psychological assessment of professional actors and related professions. *Genetic Psychology Monographs*, 1961, 64, 309–383.

Taulbee, E. S. and B. D. Sisson. Configurational analysis of MMPI profiles of psychiatric groups. *Journal of Consulting Psychology*, 1957, 21, 413–417.

Taylor, J. A. A personality scale of manifest anxiety. *Journal of Abnormal and Social Psychology*, 1953, 48, 285–290.

Urmer, A. H., H. O. Black, and L. V. Wendland. A comparison of taped and booklet forms of the Minnesota Multiphasic Personality Inventory. *Journal of Clinical Psychology*, 1960, 16, 33–34.

Wagner, E. E., and R. D. Dobbins. MMPI profiles of parishioners seeking pastoral counseling. *Journal of Consulting Psychology*, 1967, 31, 83–84.

Warman, R. E., and T. E. Hannum. MMPI pattern changes in female prisoners. *Journal of Research in Crime and Delinquency*, 1965, 2, 72–76.

Wattron, J. B. Validity of the Marsh-Hilliard-Liechti MMPI sexual deviation scale in a state prison population. *Journal of Consulting Psychology*, 1958, 22, 16.

Wauck, L. A. Schizophrenia and the MMPI. *Journal of Clinical Psychology*, 1950, 6, 279–282.

Welsh, G. S. A factor study of the MMPI using scales with item overlap eliminated. *American Psychologist*, 1952, 7, 341.

———. Factor dimensions A and R. In G. S. Welsh and W. G. Dahlstrom (Eds.), *Basic readings on the MMPI in psychology and medicine*. Minneapolis: University of Minnesota Press, 1956.

——— and W. G. Dahlstrom (Eds.). *Basic readings on the MMPI in psychology and medicine*. Minneapolis: University of Minnesota Press, 1956.

Wiener, D. N. Personality characteristics of selected disability groups. *Genetic Psychology Monographs*, 1952, 45, 175–255.

Wolf, S., W. R. Freinek, and J. W. Shaffer. Comparability of complete oral and booklet forms of the MMPI. *Journal of Clinical Psychology*, 1964, 20, 375–378.

Wolking, W. D., W. Quast, and J. J. Lawton. MMPI profiles of the parents of behaviorally disturbed children and parents from the general population. *Journal of Clinical Psychology*, 1966, 22, 39–48.

74

INDEX

Index